PENGUIN PASSNOTES

To Kill a Mockingbird

Graham Handley has taught and lectured for over thirty years. He was Principal Lecturer in English and Head of Department at the College of All Saints, Tottenham, and Research Officer in English, Birkbeck College, University of London. He is a part-time Lecturer in Literature with the University of London Department of Extramural Studies, and has examined at all levels from C.S.E. to University Honours Degree. He has published on Dickens, Mrs Gaskell and George Eliot, and has edited *The Mill on the Floss* and *Wuthering Heights* (both Macmillan) and *Daniel Deronda* (the Clarendon Press, Oxford).

PENGUIN PASSNOTES

HARPER LEE
To Kill a Mockingbird

GRAHAM HANDLEY, M.A., PH.D.
ADVISORY EDITOR: STEPHEN COOTE, M.A., PH.D.

PENGUIN BOOKS

Penguin Books Ltd, Harmondsworth, Middlesex, England
Viking Penguin Inc., 40 West 23rd Street, New York, New York 10010, U.S.A.
Penguin Books Australia Ltd, Ringwood, Victoria, Australia
Penguin Books Canada Ltd, 2801 John Street, Markham, Ontario, Canada L3R 1B4
Penguin Books (N.Z.) Ltd, 182–190 Wairau Road, Auckland 10, New Zealand

First published 1985

Excerpts from *To Kill a Mockingbird* by Harper Lee
are quoted by permission of William Heinemann Ltd.

Made and printed in Great Britain by
Richard Clay (The Chaucer Press) Ltd, Bungay, Suffolk
Filmset in Monophoto Ehrhardt by
Northumberland Press Ltd, Gateshead, Tyne and Wear

*The publishers are grateful to the following Examination Boards
for permission to reproduce questions from examination papers
used in individual titles in the Passnotes series:*

*Associated Examining Board, University of Cambridge Local Examinations
Syndicate, Joint Matriculation Board, University of London School
Examinations Department, Oxford and Cambridge Schools Examination
Board, University of Oxford Delegacy of Local Examinations.*

*The Examination Boards accept no responsibility whatsoever for the
accuracy or method of working in any suggested answers given as models.*

Contents

To the student

This book is designed to help you with your O-level or C.S.E. English Literature examinations. It contains a synopsis of the plot, a glossary of the more unfamiliar words and phrases, and a commentary on some of the issues raised by the text. An account of the writer's life is also included for background.

Page references in parentheses refer to the Pan Books edition.

When you use this book remember that it is no more than an aid to your study. It will help you find passages quickly and perhaps give you some ideas for essays. But remember: *This book is not a substitute for reading the text and it is your response and your knowledge that matter.* These are the things the examiners are looking for, and they are also the things that will give you the most pleasure. Show your knowledge and appreciation to the examiner, and show them clearly.

Introduction

NELLE HARPER LEE

Nelle Harper Lee was born in Monroeville, Alabama, on 28 April 1926, the daughter of a practising lawyer. She was educated locally, and then went to the University of Alabama to study law, later spending a year at the University of Oxford, where she was an exchange student. After a spell as an airline clerk, she submitted her first writings to a literary agent and was encouraged by the response she got, particularly to one of the stories which she later expanded into the novel we know as *To Kill a Mockingbird*. In its early form, the novel was considered by her publishers to be 'a series of short stories strung together', but Harper Lee's revisions satisfied them, and *To Kill a Mockingbird* was published in July 1960. By September of that year it was among the best-sellers, and in May 1961 Harper Lee was awarded the Pulitzer Prize for fiction. The following year the book was made into a successful film starring Gregory Peck as Atticus, and the sales of *To Kill a Mockingbird* in 1984 stand at more than 11 million.

Contemporary reviewers praised the novel's 'rare excellence', 'most authentic humor' and its imaginative identification with the 'transient world of childhood'. Scout was compared to Frankie in Carson McCullers's *The Member of the Wedding* (1946), and Harper Lee was seen as a Southern writer in the McCullers–William Faulkner tradition.

She herself spoke of *To Kill a Mockingbird* as 'a love-story pure and simple', and it is. It represents the love of childhood, of parenthood, of humanity, seen in the fight against prejudice. Its human qualities will endure.

This *Passnotes* commentary will seek to define both the novel's literary and emotional qualities and to fix its main themes and techniques firmly in the reader's mind by constant references to the text and repetition of its most significant features.

THE BACKGROUND TO THE NOVEL

The background to *To Kill a Mockingbird* is the long-term legacy of the American Civil War (1861–5), the great struggle between the Northern and Southern forces of the U.S.A. which resulted in the victory of the North and the freeing of the black slaves on the Southern plantations. The number of references to this war in the novel – through, for instance, the mention of the battle at Appomattox and various generals – show that it was very much alive in the author's mind and in the minds of her characters.

In the foreground is the town of Maycomb, readily identified with Monroeville. The period of time covered by the novel is 1933–5, a time of economic depression in the United States, as elsewhere. The small town is occasionally penetrated by news of wider issues – like the rise of Hitler and his persecution of the Jews – but essentially it lives on in its traditional assumptions of white–black segregation, its negroes being second-class citizens in the almost closed community of white supremacy.

The Confederate States – the South – had fought the North some seventy-two years before the action of the novel begins, on the issue of slavery. As we know, the South lost, but in small towns like Maycomb negroes were free only in the limited sense of being able to live in their own communities. They were still subject to the law of the whites, to racial prejudice and intolerance. They had to acquire what education they could and, in some areas, feared persecution (note the mention of the Ku Klux Klan in Chapter Fifteen). Mrs Eleanor Roosevelt, wife of the President of the United States, earns a verbal reprimand from the prejudiced Mrs Merriweather in Chapter Twenty-Four because she actually moved her chair in between the segregated blacks and whites at a meeting in Birmingham, Alabama. This evidence of a positive liberalism may help to sustain Atticus, but it cuts little ice with the Christian ladies of Maycomb.

Ironically, Birmingham, Alabama, was to be a focal point of violence twenty years later when the Civil Rights Movement – Martin Luther King's campaign to get equal rights for negroes – met irrational racial hostility of the kind that Atticus sets his face against in *To Kill a Mockingbird*.

We mentioned earlier the period of depression which is the immediate background of the novel. This was begun by the Wall Street Crash of 1929 in which billions of shares became valueless overnight. Its effects were poverty and near starvation for millions. When Roosevelt became President in 1933 he initiated the New Deal (the National Recovery Act is mentioned in Chapter Twenty-Seven) in an attempt to provide work and relieve the terrible suffering of the people. After its first effects its impetus fell away. In Chapter Two there is also a mention of the WPA (Works Progress Administration) introduced by Roosevelt in the period covered by the novel, another scheme to provide employment in the hope of maintaining the skills of working men and their own belief in themselves. The 'bread lines' are mentioned in Chapter Twelve, and these references provide an authentic historical and social setting to the novel.

These are the facts behind the fiction, but fiction has its own facts in its characters, incidents, themes and style. The main focus of this *Passnotes* commentary will be on the text itself, beginning with a synopsis of the novel.

Synopsis of To Kill a Mockingbird

The plot of *To Kill a Mockingbird* is a straightforward sequence of events recollected in maturity and set down with graphic immediacy. It is seen through the eyes of a child but is informed with the experience of its adult narrator. The location is Maycomb, a small town in Alabama in the Deep South of the United States, and the time-span of the sequence runs from the summer 'when Dill came to us' in 1933 to Halloween night, 1935.

Jean Louise Finch, whose childhood nickname was 'Scout', is the autobiographical narrator of the events, though nearly all her experiences are shared with her older brother, Jem. She also refers constantly to her father, Atticus Finch, a lawyer conspicuous for wisdom, humanity, broad tolerance and kindliness in the 'tired old town' where traditions of prejudice are faced by the first stirrings of enlightenment. Scout, Jem, and their eccentric but sensitive friend Dill – the child of a broken marriage – invent games and act plays adapted from stories, but their major fantasy is about their neighbours, the Radleys. This family of 'foot-washing Baptists' has shut itself off from friendly intercourse, an isolation even more stringently imposed since the misbehaviour of their son, Arthur, many years before. He is kept in the house and is never seen. The children pretend to think him mad and they try 'dares' in order to get him to emerge from his seclusion (pp. 19–21). They find presents in the knot-hole of a tree, undertake an excursion to the Radley home which results in Jem losing his pants (he later finds them neatly folded and repaired), and then discover that the knot-hole in the tree has been filled with cement by Mr Nathan Radley (p. 68).

The children come into contact with their other neighbours: Miss Maudie, who admires Atticus and shares much of his wisdom and enlightenment; Miss Stephanie Crawford, a leech-like gossip; and Mrs Henry Lafayette Dubose, a morphine addict who dies bravely in her attempt to break the habit (p. 116). Scout experiences school, which provides her mostly with a social education (her father's readings, standards and attitudes constitute her *real* education). She becomes more tolerant of their cook, housekeeper and substitute mother: Calpurnia. She nearly fights when a boy calls her father a nigger-defender (p. 80) and beats up her cousin Francis when he tries similar verbal baiting (p. 90). Before this, she sees snow for the first time and, more dramatically, the burning down of Miss Maudie's house (Miss Maudie hadn't cared for it much, anyway). At Christmas she visits her Aunt Alexandra (where she has her fight with Francis and is afterwards lectured in a kindly manner by her Uncle Jack). She then witnesses her father, whom she had considered 'feeble', shoot a mad dog (p. 102).

All these are 'steps' in the education of both her own feelings and Jem's. They also show the need for the children to re-adjust, to re-think their attitudes before the major event of the novel: the trial of Tom Robinson, the negro, for the alleged rape of the white girl, Mayella Ewell. The last step before that sequence begins when Jem cuts off the tops of Mrs Dubose's camellia bushes (her rudeness about Atticus provoked him) and has to read to her for punishment, with Scout in attendance (p. 112). In effect, they are watching a dying woman trying to do without morphine. Atticus has ensured that, before the ordeal to come, both children know what real courage is and don't equate it with having a gun in their hands.

The second part of the plot (pp. 119–285) consists of the prelude to the trial of the negro Tom Robinson, the trial itself, and its after-math. Atticus has been briefed to defend Tom Robinson. His self-respect and his need to maintain his esteem in his children's eyes won't let him turn the case down, though the effects of it are to change all their lives. Before the trial, Scout is instrumental in dispersing a gang of local men (one of whom is Walter Cunningham's father) who are threatening Atticus and trying to lynch Tom Robinson (pp. 157–8). Although by now the children are being looked after by Aunt Alexandra, Atticus's younger sister, they manage to see most of the trial sitting in the gallery with the negroes. (They had previously visited the negro church with Calpurnia.) As they watch and listen, they realize even more fully than before the nature of their father's integrity, his respect for the law, and his dedication to a wider unwritten law: the ideal of humanity, the ideal of justice regardless of colour, creed or way of life. They then watch how Atticus's skill in cross-examination establishes Tom Robinson's innocence (pp. 178–93). (Dill and Jem respond even more emotionally to this than Scout.) Nonetheless, the white jury convicts the black man who is sent to a prison farm pending an appeal (p. 223). The father of the 'raped' girl, Bob Ewell, humiliated by Atticus (perhaps because guilty of the rape and violence himself), vows vengeance on Atticus and his family. Jem and Scout become apprehensive on their father's account. Coached by Aunt Alexandra, Scout attends the missionary tea party with a ladylike mien (p. 231), but Atticus brings news that Tom Robinson, trying to escape, has been shot seventeen times by the guards (p. 239). Atticus, accompanied by Calpurnia, goes to tell Helen Robinson of her husband's death. After threatening her, Judge Taylor and Atticus, Bob Ewell continues along his path of revenge. On the Halloween night of Mrs Merriweather's Maycomb pageant, Bob Ewell attacks Scout and Jem on their way home (p. 266). Jem's arm is broken and only the chicken wire around Scout's 'ham' costume saves her from serious injury. However, their more immediate rescuer, unknown to the children, is none other than the mysterious Boo (Arthur) Radley. He pulls Bob Ewell off Scout, kills him, and carries the injured Jem back to the house. Heck Tate, the sheriff, removes the knife that Ewell had, and covers up the whole incident by suggesting that Ewell killed himself (Atticus at first believed that Jem had killed him). Tate, obviously influenced by Atticus's character and conduct at the trial, establishes the hope for simple human justice by asserting 'There's a black boy dead for no reason, and the man responsible for it's dead' (p. 280). The children have clearly been mistaken about Boo. His little gestures of friendship culminate in the great gesture of rescue. Scout, the little child, takes this big and timid child home. She then stands on the Radley porch for a moment and reviews all the events they have lived through.

There is a naturalness and subtlety about the presentation of the characters in the book. They all display an unforced adherence to truth. They are real in reaction, in psychological consistency and in their responses to their respective situations. For example, Scout and Jem acquire an increased awareness of change within themselves, whether it be in the oncoming of adolescence, or new knowledge of their father (he was once 'one-shot Finch'), or a new attitude as a result of their visit to the church with Calpurnia. Thus, *To Kill a Mockingbird* is a novel which records deftly and deeply part of the process of growing up. Fantasy gives way to reality, imagination to recognition, misconception to new understanding. The education of the children in life is contrasted with the sterile and unrelated education of school. In the latter, the emphasis is on facts as distinct from the reality of living in the real world or the world of the imagination. Here there are clear points of contact between Harper Lee and her great humanitarian predecessor, Charles Dickens, whose novel *Hard Times* (1854) also attacked the stultifying nature of a classroom instruction which equated education with the meaningless acquisition of facts, facts which bore no relation to feelings, imagination, or life.

In *To Kill a Mockingbird* education in social awareness – and this means moral awareness, too – is pre-eminent. Teacher discussion with the class can evaluate the anti-humanitarian actions of Hitler in his persecution of the Jews (p. 248), but only movement into the small, divided society of Maycomb can show the children the anti-humanitarian prejudice of white man against black on their own doorstep. The lives of the children are thus placed in an immediate local context and also a much wider one: the mid-thirties in America, a time of economic depression. President Roosevelt's new deal, his package of reforms designed to combat the worst effects of the depression after the Wall Street collapse of 1929, have their effects in Maycomb County. Scout learns from her father of the poverty of the farmers and sees in Walter Cunningham, Burris Ewell and his family, poverty, filth and loneliness, those breeders of hate, violence and greed. Thus Maycomb, in its rural way, mirrors a wider suffering, just as its trial and the results of that mirror the wider instances of man's persecution of man.

Yet, as the plot develops, so a tone of gradual optimism evolves. Although 'the mockingbird' of the trial – Tom Robinson – is condemned and later judicially murdered, 'the mockingbird' of the shadows – Boo Radley – rescues and is preserved. Tolerance, understanding, humanity are all making their way in the small and circumscribed community of Maycomb, and if Atticus is the standard bearer, then Miss Maudie is of the advanced guard. Mr Underwood's uncompromising post-trial verdict, Heck Tate's own rough equation of justice which shelters Boo Radley – all these show that the forces of humanity are assembling to destroy the traditions and practice of white–black inequality. The final note sounded is as optimistic, as free as the song of the mockingbird itself. And that bird has his third human parallel in Atticus, whose own song is the great Christian one of the brotherhood of man.

But if the plot is serious, it is also irradiated by a delightful, running humour and balanced by moments of poignancy and pathos. Think of Dill's and Jem's lie after the children have penetrated the Radley garden and Jem has left his pants on the wire, having supposedly gambled them away at strip-poker; or Scout falling asleep at the Maycomb pageant, making her very late entry as a ham and thus causing Judge Taylor to double up with laughter and Mrs Merriweather to act the tragedy queen. Think of Jem then finding his pants, of the children examining the knot-hole for further presents and finding replicas of themselves. Consider Scout finding the blanket around her shoulders, placed there (unknown to her) by that same prisoner Boo Radley as she watches the burning of Miss Maudie's house in the freezing cold.

The plot is also heightened by moments of sheer drama, perhaps the best of these being the tensely atmospheric sequence, full of foreboding and climaxed by violence, as Bob Ewell follows and then attacks Scout and Jem.

Within the movement of the plot there is a superb sense of balance, an ability to switch from satirical verve – the account of the ladies' missionary tea, for example – to immediate, real happenings, as when Atticus interrupts this tea with the news of the killing of Tom Robinson. Experience of life and reality replaces the chatter of the pompous 'Christian' ladies who are bigoted, intolerant and hypocritical. Atticus proceeds to immediate Christian and practical action – taking Calpurnia with him – by trying to help Helen Robinson as the ladies talk on in their protected world of social gossip and religiosity, removed from reality by the refinements of being white.

Finally and unobtrusively, Atticus, Miss Maudie and the children themselves on the night of the attack remind us of the binding symbol of the mockingbird, the symbol that says that what is natural is right, what is unnatural is wrong. The bird sings freely, but man is only free when he comes to recognize that humanity knows no colour, that prejudice must be rooted out and that progress is achieved by sacrifice and example.

An Account of the Plot

PART ONE

Chapter One (*pp. 9–21*)

The first-person narrator, soon to be known to us as 'Scout', looks back to the time when her brother Jem, then nearly thirteen, broke his arm. She considers that the events leading to it originated with the Ewells, but Jem himself puts the incident down to the arrival of their friend Dill (Charles Baker Harris) one summer, and his idea of making 'Boo Radley come out' (p. 9).

Scout then traces the Southern line of the Finches through one Simon, who established the Finch clan and died rich. Scout next gives an account of her father, Atticus Finch, who left the homestead at Finch's Landing and went to Montgomery, Alabama, to read law, returning to Maycomb to practise it. He pays for his younger brother's education, settles in the 'tired old town' (p. 11), and Scout recalls distinctly the slow pace of life there during the depression. She describes their negro cook Calpurnia, with whom she bickers but who has taken the place of their dead mother.

The major recollection of the chapter is the arrival of Dill – 'I'm little but I'm old' (p. 13) – that summer. He has white hair, a vivid imagination, and has had experiences, like seeing *Dracula*, that command the children's respect. He enters their dramas, his precocious imagination enriching their own. He also directs their obsessions towards their neighbours, the Radleys. Their house and its inmates are invested with local suspicions and fears. The family has always kept itself to itself, unlike most people in Maycomb. The 'neighbourhood legend' (p. 15) has it that the youngest boy Arthur was part of a gang of youths who went around creating trouble. He, with the other boys, was brought before the judge but, unlike the others (who had a good education at the industrial school), he was released to his father's custody and has not been seen for fifteen years. He is known as Boo, and there are a number of stories about him. When his father dies, Boo's elder brother Nathan comes to take charge of the house. He is reticent, but does speak to the children. Jem's vivid and fanciful description of Boo further excites Dill's already over-active imagination, and he suggests that they direct their attention to making Boo Radley 'come out'. He dares Jem to try, eventually settling for his just touching the house. Although sneered at by Scout, Jem does this. The children run away, but think they saw 'an inside shutter move' (p. 21).

This is a fine opening chapter, setting the time and the place against the background of history, and making the transition easily and naturally into childhood experience. The account of Atticus's first case has an ironically humorous flavour, while the descriptions of Maycomb, Atticus and Calpurnia are drily funny but warm. There is a natural simplicity in the dialogue between the children. It is racy, unforced and colloquial. The story of the Radleys, however, evokes an atmosphere of mystery and fear. Remember that the whole is seen through the eyes of an imaginative adult recollecting with clarity and perspective things as they were.

The perceptive reader will also notice a subtly ironic note at the very beginning of the chapter (p. 9) when we are told that Jem's left arm was somewhat shorter than his right. He has not been incapacitated permanently by Bob Ewell, but the negro Tom Robinson (whose withered left arm was testimony to his innocence) was condemned and later shot as a result of Ewell's lies.

Chapter Two (*pp. 21–8*)

Dill leaves at the end of the summer, and Scout starts school, Jem having been given some pocket money by Atticus to ensure that he takes her there. Scout gives a delightful description of her teacher, Miss Caroline Fisher ('She looked and smelled like a peppermint drop', p. 22) and a satirical account of her teaching methods. Miss Caroline tells Scout to inform Atticus that he mustn't teach her any more because he doesn't know how to teach as the system requires. Scout broods on this, confides in Jem and gets into worse trouble with Miss Fisher by demonstrating that she can indeed read and write, her competence having been fostered by the tasks which Calpurnia set her.

Scout's social education is extended when Miss Fisher finds that Walter Cunningham has brought no lunch with him and that he will not accept money to get any. Scout has to point out to Miss Fisher that despite their poverty the Cunninghams are so independent that they don't accept anything without paying it back. She has learned this from Atticus's dealing with Walter's father, for the latter paid in goods – hickory nuts and turnip greens – for Atticus's advice. Atticus explained to her then how the economic depression had hit the farmers, but Scout has not yet acquired the ease of expression which enables her to put this convincingly to Miss Fisher, who lightly canes her on the hand, to the general amusement of the class. When Scout leaves for lunch, she sees that Miss Fisher has buried her head in her arms.

The narrative conveys Scout's excitement at the thought of going to school, her disillusionment with her experiences there, and pinpoints her sharp awareness of Jem's condescending manner, which is the beginning of a shift in their relationship. Though Scout describes Miss Fisher with satirical verve, she is aware that Jem's adolescent pangs began when he saw her. Miss Fisher's unsuitable story and the reaction it provokes (p. 22) show the gap between theory and reality. Her limitations – and the limitations of the educational system – are shown when she reveals her distaste for Scout's literacy, saying 'It's best to begin reading with a fresh mind' (p. 23).

Scout's own satirical and ironic comments punctuate the chapter, but most moving is her identification, in respect and love, with her father ('I crawled into his lap every night', p. 24) and the poignant 'Until I feared I would lose it, I never loved to read. One does not love breathing' (p. 24). This is both wise and economical, typical of Harper Lee's style throughout. It is reinforced by sharply phrased sarcasm (as when Scout refers to the Dewey Decimal System as 'impressionistic revelations', p. 24).

There is social and moral comment in the descriptions of Walter Cunningham (he has no shoes but does have hookworm), and we see Miss Fisher as the outsider in a community in which everyone knows everyone else, their needs and their peculiarities. At the back of this is the wider perspective of poverty in the period, but the immediate facts of it are Walter's deprivation. Scout's courage in speaking on his behalf anticipates her courage when she speaks to the men who have come to lynch Tom Robinson, one of whom is Walter's father. The lack of understanding shown by Miss Fisher anticipates the wider lack of understanding later in the book, the failure to see that tolerance and humility are the roots of understanding and humanity. There is genuine pathos at the end of the chapter with Miss Fisher's abject gesture of her own – and the educational system's – failure.

Chapter Three (*pp. 29–38*)

Scout rubs Walter's nose in the dirt, but is stopped by Jem, who invites him home to dinner. He accepts, since Jem says that their fathers are friends. They pass the Radley house – Jem is in boastful mood – and get home, where Atticus engages Walter in conversation about crops. When they are eating Scout exclaims at Walter's pouring syrup over his vegetables, but is silently reprimanded by Atticus and verbally lashed for her bad manners by Calpurnia. Another aspect of her social and moral education has begun, and she finishes her dinner in the kitchen above, smarting from the humiliation and vowing to 'fix' Calpurnia. She complains about her to Atticus whose voice is 'flinty' when he tells her that he has no intention of getting rid of Calpurnia.

Scout returns to school and faces another crisis: Miss Fisher's discovery of a 'cootie' in Burris Ewell's hair. Her social education is beginning. Scout describes the boy's filthiness, and learns that he only attends for the first day of each term, since the 'truant lady' has not found the means to keep him there. He is angered by the teacher's attempt to exert her authority over him, but Little Chuck Little saves the situation by threatening Burris. The latter leaves, abusing Miss Caroline. The class gather round to comfort their crying teacher. She responds by reading them *Toad of Toad Hall*, and Scout, her illusions about school shattered, thinks about running away. She is somewhat softened when she finds that Calpurnia has missed them both and has made some crackling bread. In the evening Scout tells Atticus that she doesn't wish to continue at school, but Atticus teaches her the simple trick of how to get on with people: you must consider things from their point of view. He tells her the fact that you don't really comprehend anyone until 'you climb into his skin and walk around in it' (p. 35). Scout responds with the example of Burris Ewell. If she followed his example she wouldn't have to go to school at all. Atticus then distinguishes between 'common folk' like himself and Scout, and the Ewells, who 'lived like animals', the father spending his money on green whisky while the children starved. Atticus and Scout reach a compromise, a confidential one in which he will continue reading and she will carry on going to school.

Vivid language and sustained dialect mark the early part of this chapter. Walter looked 'as if he had been raised on fish food' (p. 29), while Jem informs Walter that a 'haint' lives at the Radley house (p. 29). Calpurnia teaches Scout good manners to a guest and there is a humour she is unaware of in her words: 'if he wants to eat up the table cloth you let him, you hear?' (p. 30). Scout further learns of her father's respect for Calpurnia. The humanitarian note (the belief in the equality and worth of all people) is being firmly struck. Atticus practises what he preaches, and equality begins in his own home. The incident with Burris Ewell and Miss Caroline antici- pates the 'contentious' or logical and argumentative nature of the father later on, but the filth of the boy, his abuse and his potential violence, are squarely laid at the door of the social conditions which have pro- duced them. They are not his own fault. Little Chuck Little's threat to kill Burris underlines the pathos of all those who live in poverty. There is tension here, a strong sense of community in the comforting of the teacher, and a clear insight into Scout's changing reactions throughout this eventful day.

Atticus's phrase about getting inside another's skin is the moral pivot of the whole novel, for Scout's growing awareness through experience – and the awareness which Atticus fosters by the example of others – turns on his concept of sympathy with other people. In this way prejudice and its evils will be overcome. Atticus's lawyer's gifts for rational argument – and compromises – are seen on the domestic level of understanding his own child, but they suggest the intellectual and humanitarian commitment he brings to the defence of Tom Robinson in court.

There is also much humour here; for example, we are shown Jem spending an entire Saturday in the treehouse.

Chapter Four (*pp. 38–47*)

Scout's satirical account of the 'remainder of her schooldays', with its Projects and Units, leaves her with the feeling that she has been cheated, for her real education has come from her father, from books, and *Time* magazine rather than school.

She soon switches to a significant event, the discovery of some Wrigley's Double-Mint in the knot-hole of an oak outside the Radley house. Scout chews it, but is made to gargle afterwards by the suspicious Jem. The next day they discover 'Indian-heads' in the same place, and adopt the accepted code of 'finders keepers'. Two days later Dill comes for the summer, says he smells death as he looks at the Radley Place, and learns about 'Hot Steams' from Jem. Scout contradicts Jem's version, and is the first into the tyre which rolls out of control to the steps of the Radley Place. Scout gets out and runs back, leaving the tyre, and the children drink lemonade. Jem suggests that they play a game called 'Boo Radley'. It turns into a play, dramatically polished and improved and changed throughout the summer. For Scout it is an experience of love and fear, but Jem assures her that Boo Radley won't get her because he is dead. One day Atticus sees them enacting their Radley drama, suspects what is going on but says nothing to stop them. Scout, sensitively aware that he disapproves, opts out of the play. She also reveals that when she rolled into the Radley Place in the tyre she heard someone laughing inside the house.

The attack on stereotyped as distinct from real education as Scout 'inched sluggishly along the treadmill' of the state system is continued. Soon, however, they find another present in the tree, an unobtrusive indication of the real Boo Radley's concern and affection for the children he only sees. Before the next present of the 'Indian-heads' there is a lyrical description of summer, 'a thousand colours in a parched landscape' (p. 40). The 'finders keepers' right is ironically described by Scout as 'part of our ethical culture' (p. 41), but Jem's superstitious nature plays fully on the magic significance of the 'Indian-heads'.

There is pathos in Dill's transformation – new clothes can't compensate for having no real home – but his imaginative flair is unimpaired, though the children's first game with the tyres in fact strengthens Scout's fears and apprehensions about the Radleys.

Colloquial or everyday language continues to be the main ingredient of an unforced and natural style. This may be contrasted to the highly imaginative use of language, as when Jem describes 'Hot Steams', or Scout, whirling in the tyre, describes the 'mad palette of ground, sky and houses' (pp. 42–3). This latter incident is dramatic and frightening, and the superbly imaginative Radley dramas contain plenty of humour as well as macabre emphases, like Boo biting off his mother's forefinger 'when he couldn't find any cats and squirrels to eat' (p. 45). The world of imaginative childhood exploration is captured naturally in Scout's participations, her fears, her sensitive response to Atticus's unvoiced criticism, and her own apprehension, revealed in a masterly dramatic stroke at the very end of the chapter, thus maintaining the reader's involvement in the mystery.

Chapter Five (*pp. 47–55*)

Jem agrees to tone down the Radley game. Scout is annoyed with Dill, who proposes to her and then forgets about it. She is aware that Jem and Dill turn to one another and exclude her because she is a girl. Next she lovingly describes Miss Maudie ('a chameleon lady', p. 48), but shows a strong eye for realism too. Miss Maudie makes the finest cakes for the children, and Scout shares evenings with her on her porch. She questions her about Boo Radley – Miss Maudie assures her that he is alive – and then recounts her Uncle Jack's loud proposals to Miss Maudie in order to defend him against the woman's sharp teasing. Miss Maudie explains that the Radleys and their like are 'foot-washing' Baptists who believe that pleasure is a sin, and Scout reveals that she and Jem regard Miss Maudie as a friend despite her acid tongue. Miss Maudie dismisses the rumours about Arthur, praises Atticus, is satirical about the neighbourhood do-gooder Miss Stephanie Crawford, and speaks of the Radleys' as 'a sad house' (p. 51). Next day Jem reveals dramatically that they are going to give a note to Boo Radley, an idea greeted with apprehension and horror by Scout. They get a bamboo pole and go down to the house, put the note on the end of the pole, but it flutters to the ground. Dill rings the bell, Atticus sees what they are up to, and tells them to leave the Radleys alone. His tone is severe, and he says that they have been 'putting his [Arthur's] life history on display' (p. 55). Jem, humiliated, tricked by his father's insight, shouts after him that he's not sure he wants to be a lawyer now.

The twin focus of this chapter is on the character of Miss Maudie and Atticus's deliberately moral stance over the Boo Radley game. The whole chapter is concerned with the developing experiences of the children and what they learn from them. We see Scout in relation to Dill and Jem, Miss Maudie's truth-telling as antidote to rumours, her kindness to the children, her valuation of Atticus (which is the same as the reader's), her wonderful retort to Uncle Jack's proposal, 'they'll hear you at the post office' (p. 49), her brushes with the narrow Baptist sect. Above all, Miss Maudie's reaction to Stephanie Crawford's finding Arthur (Boo) looking in her room at night – 'what did you do, Stephanie, move over in the bed and make room for him?' (p. 51) – punctures that complacent rumourmonger. The attempt to deliver a letter to a side window of the Radley house is done with graphic immediacy, the reactions of each child conveying the mounting tension which makes Atticus's arrival the perfect climax, for although he's not 'Boo Radley and his bloody fangs' (p. 54) his language, cleverly offered in reported speech, has a rhetorical ring characteristic of the good lawyer and typical of the good man. Jem's education is also furthered by the experience of being outmanoeuvred.

Chapter Six (*pp. 56–63*)

It is Dill's last night in Maycomb, so the children are allowed to sit with him by Miss Rachel's pool. They see Mr Avery urinating, unaware that they are watching him. They later walk away, telling Scout she can go home if she wants to, but they are intent on looking into the Radley house. Scout accompanies them and they get under the wire fence and approach the house first from the back, then from the side. Dill looks in but can see nothing.

Jem moves to the back, and Scout sees the shadow of a man approaching him. The children run and Scout trips as a shotgun is fired. They get back through the wire, but Jem has to leave his pants hanging on it in order to free himself. When they arrive in their street they find Mr Nathan holding a shotgun. The neighbours tell them that he shot a negro in his collard patch, and they immediately notice the absence of Jem's pants. Dill, earlier accused by Scout of being a liar, rises to the occasion by 'hatching one' (p. 60) which saves them, asserting that he won Jem's pants when they played strip-poker with matches. Jem goes off to Dill's, supposedly to get his pants, while Atticus smooths things down with Miss Rachel. Later that night, when everyone except Scout is asleep, Jem goes to retrieve his pants from the wire. He has to fight Scout before he can do so, but returns with them safely.

This chapter moves from the humour of the children observing Mr Avery's nocturnal practice to the tension of the attempt to see into the Radleys' house, the fear evoked by seeing the shadow of the man, the fleeing and the sound of the shotgun, the affectedly non-chalant return to the main street, Dill's superbly explanatory lie, his kissing Scout, and Jem's brave recovery of the pants from the Radley wire. It is taut narrative throughout, filled with the atmosphere of daring and fear, the darkness, sounds, acute observation (note the description of the Radley porch), figurative language (the shadow is 'crisp as toast', p. 59), the chorus of neighbours (Miss Stephanie ominously refers to a 'white nigger', p. 60) and the continuing 'education' of the children. We see Scout's realization of the danger to Jem and her anguished wait for his return, and Jem's new-found maturity and courage. He also gains the knowledge that they shouldn't have done what they did and a recognition of his father's essential rightness of standards.

Chapter Seven (*pp. 63–9*)

Scout decides not to bother Jem, and soon she is in the second grade at school. It is as bad as the first, but one day, walking home with Jem, she learns that when he retrieved his pants they were neatly folded on the fence, as if somebody knew he would be returning. The next thing is that they find a ball of twine in the knot-hole. Jem eventually takes it, and they discover two 'small images carved in soap' of a boy and a girl (p. 65). These represent Jem and Scout, and the latter is scared, despite their beauty. Later they find chewing-gum and what Atticus describes as a spelling-medal, then a pocket-watch (which doesn't work). Jem ponders on whether they should confide in Atticus, but the children decide to write a thank you letter and place it in the knot-hole the next morning. When Jem gets there, followed by Scout, they find that the knot-hole has been plugged with cement. Jem asks Mr Nathan why this should be and is told that the tree is dying. He asks Atticus if this is so, and is told that it isn't true. Atticus adds that Mr Nathan knows more about his trees than they do. Later Scout finds that Jem has been crying.

This chapter deepens the mystery of Boo Radley, first with Jem's revelation about the repaired and folded pants, and then with the appearance of the gifts in the knot-hole. Jem's 'Egyptian Period' is ironically described – he is very much the kind of boy who has obsessional fancies from time to time – but this gives way to his lawyer-like investigation of the presents they receive, his questioning of Atticus about the spelling-medal, his writing of the thank you letter. All of these reveal a deepening sensitivity and awareness. He is protective over Scout, urging her not to cry about the cement, has the courage to question Mr Nathan, then his father – he is developing as a young lawyer! – while his tears surely indicate that he half knows the truth: that the presents are from the lonely 'boy' within. They are his only contact with the outside world in which he can never live. There is a directness about the dialogue of question and answer which foreshadows the court scene to come. It is a domestic equivalent of trying to find out the truth and being moved by suffering.

Chapter Eight (*pp. 69–80*)

Old Mrs Radley dies, and there is an exceptionally cold winter. Scout sees snow for the first time. School is cancelled (it is the first snow since 1885), Mr Avery accuses them of changing the seasons, and Miss Maudie says they can take as much snow as they like. All she is concerned with is protecting her flowers. Meanwhile, Scout and Jem construct a snowman, Jem shaping it like Mr Avery. When Atticus returns, though he compliments Jem, he says he has 'perpetrated a near libel' (p. 73) and suggests they alter the snowman somewhat. Jem takes Miss Maudie's hat and hedge-clippers, adorning the snowman with them, and thus constructing what they hear is 'an absolute morphodite in that yard' (p. 74). 'Morphodite' is colloquial for 'hermaphrodite' which means having the characteristics of both genders. Scout is woken in the middle of the night to be told by Atticus that Miss Maudie's house is on fire. The children watch the blaze from in front of the Radley place as furniture is removed, and then see the fire spreading towards their own house. Atticus remains calm – 'He might have been watching a football game' (p. 76). Miss Maudie's house burns down (she didn't like it anyway) and when the children arrive back home Atticus notices that Scout has a blanket round her shoulders. With this revelation, Jem pours out all his thoughts about Mr Nathan, but Atticus says they should keep quiet about it, and that Boo Radley put the blanket around Scout, whose stomach 'turned to water' (p. 78) when she heard this. The next day the children take back Miss Maudie's things, and find that she is not grieving for the loss of her house. She is thinking of them and of others. She is reduced to laughter when they say they can rake up the 'Morphodite' 'in a jiffy' (p. 80).

The chapter opens with a satirical glance at Mr Avery and his judgements (it is reinforced by another glance later) and then the snow arrives ('The *world*'s endin'', p. 70). It is soon used by the children in one of their games. They make a caricature snowman converted soon into an hermaphrodite by Jem's inventive facility. The description conveys the children's energy, enthusiasm and humour, together with the humour that Atticus himself sees in the original, which has to be altered because of its libellous suggestions. Trust Atticus to think in legal terms! But the humour quickly changes to drama with the burning of Miss Maudie's house and the fear of the fire spreading. Atticus, protective and calm, continues to grow in stature as a character, as does Miss Maudie, who surveys the burning almost with serenity. There are grotesque elements in the breakdown of the fire-engine, in Mr Avery's descent into Miss Maudie's shrubbery, in the crumbling of the 'Absolute Morphodite', but there is also dramatic tension in the activities of the half-dressed men battling to contain the fire with hand extinguishers and blankets. The drama continues when Scout's blanket is discovered and Jem becomes nearly hysterical over Mr Nathan. Miss Maudie's reactions afterwards, her plans for the future, and her concern for others, all show that she is imbued with the same kind of humanity as Atticus. Seeing her hands 'brown with dirt and dried blood' (p. 80) Jem asks her 'Why don't you get a coloured man?', a reminder of the subordinate role of the blacks in Maycomb.

Chapter Nine (*pp. 80–94*)

After an exchange with Cecil Jacobs, Scout gets her father to explain why he is defending a negro. Atticus replies that he couldn't expect them to obey him any more if he didn't, he would lose their respect, and he urges Scout to 'Try fighting with your head for a change' (p. 81). He also tells her that they are not going to win, that they will be fighting their friends, but that when things get bad to remember that 'they're still our friends, and this is still our home' (p. 82).

Christmas arrives, and Atticus and the children go to Finch's Landing to stay with Aunt Alexandra, Atticus's sister, and her grandson, Francis. First Atticus's younger brother Jack, the doctor, comes to join them. He has a good sense of humour, and Scout obviously likes him, though he objects to her use of the word 'damn', and is obviously worried by her tomboyish qualities. The next day the children get presents of air rifles from Atticus, and Finch's Landing is described, together with the more humorous aspects of Finch history associated with it.

Francis is 'the most boring child I have ever met' (p. 87) according to Scout, a tell-tale and boaster, while Aunt Alexandra is obsessed with Scout's clothes and with her becoming a lady, implying that she doesn't hold out much hope of that with Atticus letting her go around in overalls. At dinner Scout has to sit apart. Afterwards she tells Francis she is going to marry Dill, and she takes his mockery until he calls Atticus a 'nigger-lover' and accuses him of ruining the family. Scout stalks him, eventually catches up with him and splits her knuckle 'to the bone' on his front teeth (p. 90). Francis lies, Atticus, Jack and the other children leave, and Scout, after 'reflecting upon relativity' (p. 91), tells Uncle Jack her side of the incident. When he hears it he is intent upon bringing the facts to Alexandra's notice. Later Scout creeps downstairs and listens to Atticus and Uncle Jack discussing her, the bringing up of children, and the coming trial, with Atticus saying that he hopes he can get 'Jem and Scout through it without bitterness' (p. 94). Many years later she realizes that Atticus wanted her to hear every word he said.

Scout experiences the first taste of what it means for her father to be defending a negro against a white man. Her small worry of trying to get off school by catching ringworm gives way to her larger concern to hear Atticus's explanation (p. 81). She hears more than that, for he advises moderation, a check on Scout's impulsive tendencies. Aware of the seriousness, Scout crawls into his lap, always her way of expressing her insecurity and need for love. Scout conquers her feelings temporarily, but they rise again into explosive action when Francis taunts her about Atticus. The chapter is full of vivid family insights, word-pictures of relations like Uncle Jack – kind, a joker, not really understanding children – Aunt Alexandra, 'analogous to Mount Everest ... she was cold and there' (p. 83). Scout becomes aware that she is supposed to grow up to be a lady, and gives a wonderfully satirical account of Finch history at the landing before proceeding to outline Francis's character and that of his grandmother. The narrative bristles with description, dialogue, impending action, and it centres on Scout's assault on Francis and the sudden return home. It shows that Scout cannot really curb her impetuosity, but also that she will not descend to Francis's level and tell tales. There is a delightful exchange between her and Uncle Jack when he bathes her damaged knuckle, and an even more poignant and pathetic one between Atticus and Uncle Jack. The latter, for all his good humour, doesn't understand children sufficiently. He falls back on literary or historical analogy, whereas Atticus is tolerant, understands phases in growing up like the use of bad language, and concentrates on the really serious things of life, like the exposure of children to the prejudice they will meet in the coming weeks.

Chapter Ten (*pp. 95–104*)

Atticus, nearly fifty, is described in order to show that he doesn't do the same things as the parents of Scout's and Jem's school friends. He instructs them not to shoot at mockingbirds with their air rifles and Miss Maudie explains that this is because mockingbirds 'sing their hearts out for us' (p. 96). They are symbols of naturalness, generosity and kindness. She tells Scout of all the things that Atticus can do – Scout is not convinced – and Atticus later reprimands Scout for pointing her gun at Miss Maudie. Atticus refuses to take part in the Methodist football match against the Baptists, but his moment arrives when the mad dog Tim Johnson enters the town. Spotted by Jem and Scout, it walks lopsidedly. Cal phones Atticus and then runs to warn the neighbours. The dog comes down the deserted street – 'the mockingbirds were silent' (p. 100) – and the children are amazed when the sheriff, Heck Tate, hands the gun to Atticus. At first Atticus declines, but then he 'moved like an underwater swimmer' (p. 102), his glasses slip down into the street, and he shoots the dog dead. Miss Maudie emerges to call Atticus 'One-Shot Finch', Heck Tate appears about to refer to his reputation in the past, but Atticus silences him and warns Jem not to go near the dog. Jem, almost inarticulate and obviously proud, talks to Scout, and Miss Maudie tells the children just what a first-rate shot their father is. Scout wants to let everyone know about it, but Jem counsels silence on Atticus's past glory, saying that if he'd wanted them to know he would have told them.

This chapter sounds the major themes of the novel. It demonstrates that what appears to be is not always true. This is important in high-lighting the main theme of man's inhumanity and prejudice. For instance, Atticus is unlike the other parents. He is apparently 'feeble', but he shows that he is exceptional in a crisis and that he commands a rare skill. This revelation that things and people are not always what they seem gives Scout and Jem new insights into Atticus's charac-ter.

The emphatic 'it's a sin to kill a mockingbird' (p. 96) is the first reference to the symbol which is later to permeate the action of the novel. It represents natural freedom and goodness. Miss Maudie takes it up immediately. The symbol of the mockingbird extends into a number of areas, but embraces the two central 'mockingbirds' who injure no one and lead good and loving lives: Arthur Radley and Tom Robinson. Both are 'shot', the first by the hunters of gossip, the second physically by prejudice and the bullets of the guards.

Atticus's modesty, integrity, and natural apprehension are all stressed in this chapter, and the children come to understand the code he lives by and what he hopes from them. The tension is superbly maintained, not merely through visual description, but through the brief and hurried dialogue and the initial panic of trying to warn everyone, followed by the sheriff's deferring to Atticus to undertake what should be his own job. Figurative language throughout is, as usual, telling. Vivid strokes, generally from nature, convey the imaginative feelings of the narrator. The children see the dog 'shiver like a horse shedding fleas', for instance (p. 101).

Again, Miss Maudie is the moral centre of the action, filling in gaps for the children, and truly evaluating for them the quality of their father. What Jem has learned is apparent from the end of the chapter. This time there is no shouting after his father. Scout's own imagination is shown again as her father goes into the middle of the street to shoot the dog and she thinks – 'he moved like an underwater swimmer' (p. 102). This imaginative description will be recalled later (in Chapter Twenty-One) when the jury come in and Scout sees them as 'moving like underwater swimmers' (p. 215). Immediately afterwards she recalls Atticus walking into the street with the rifle.

Chapter Eleven (*pp. 105–18*)

This last chapter of Part One opens with a description of Mrs Henry Lafayette Dubose and shows why the children hate her. She has a vicious tongue, and Jem is frequently infuriated by her innuendo. Atticus counsels tolerance and is always extravagantly polite to Mrs Dubose. One afternoon, when Jem and Scout are returning from town, Jem has an unpleasant exchange with Mrs Dubose, whose abuse includes an attack on Atticus for 'lawing for niggers!' (p. 107). Jem is generally easy-going, but this time he rises to the bait and later cuts off all the tops of Mrs Dubose's camellia bushes. He also smashes Scout's baton, but Scout realizes that he is suffering. Atticus learns of the incident and tells Jem to go and apologize. After he leaves, Scout crawls into Atticus's lap. He talks to her about the Tom Robinson case, warns of the suffering to come, and tells her the fundamental truth that 'The one thing that doesn't abide by majority rule is a person's conscience' (pp. 110–11). Jem returns to say that as a punishment Mrs Dubose wants him to read to her regularly for a month. When he says that the place is creepy Atticus tells him: 'Just pretend you're inside the Radley house' (p. 111).

The children visit Mrs Dubose, and Scout describes in detail the room and, in particular, the revolting physical condition of Mrs Dubose herself. We are shown her suffering as well as her sharpness. The sessions continue, with Mrs Dubose regularly referring to Atticus as a 'nigger-lover'. Scout asks Atticus if he is such, and he replies that he does his best 'to love everybody' (p. 114). Each afternoon Mrs Dubose passes into a kind of fit, but she greets Atticus warmly when he arrives during one of the readings. Jem's reading is extended by Atticus, but finally the children escape. One evening, Atticus returns to tell them of Mrs Dubose's death, and of how she was able to break the morphine habit because of Jem's readings to her. She has bequeathed him a camellia. Jem responds hysterically, but Atticus explains that he wanted him to see what 'real courage is, instead of getting the idea that courage is a man with a gun in his hand' (p. 119).

This chapter acts as a fine contrast to the preceding one. It concentrates on real suffering, and picks up the theme that things are often not what they appear to be. Atticus is continuing the education of his children, and Scout unconsciously anticipates a phrase which Atticus is to echo about Mrs Dubose – 'my father, who hated guns ... was the bravest man who ever lived' (p. 106). This is ironic in view of Atticus's later definition of Mrs Dubose's bravery as she asserts her independence of everyone by rejecting the morphine which has eased her for so long. It is doubly ironic that Jem and Scout are the unknowing instruments who enable her to do it. The reality of the Dubose interior and of Mrs Dubose herself are sordid but poignant, the onset of the fits and the alarm clock going off later every day maintaining narrative tension. That tension is present in Jem's reaction in cutting up the camellias, and at the end in his reaction that Mrs Dubose is speaking from beyond the grave by giving him the camellia. And in the background, carefully inserted in between the visits, is the knowledge of what is going to occur in the future. This education in suffering is a preparation for a greater suffering to come, but the immediacy of this is also a prelude to a wider understanding of people and their needs. Atticus's appraisal of Mrs Dubose – 'She was the bravest person I ever knew' (p. 118) – is a conscious invitation to his children to embrace independence of conscience, charity and humanity in the crisis to come. There are the usual vivid and evocative phrases – 'wet ... inched like a glacier', p. 112 – and 'Her mouth seemed to have a private existence of its own ... like a clam hole at low tide', p. 113.

PART TWO

Chapter Twelve (*pp. 119–30*)

Jem is now twelve, moody, and tells Scout that she ought to start behaving like a girl. Scout turns to Calpurnia and then learns that Dill is not coming for the summer, though he vows eternal devotion to her. Outside the country is growing poorer, Atticus attends the state legislature for two weeks, and Calpurnia decides to take the children to her church. The latter, the cemetery, and the whole atmosphere of their visit are described, and though one woman opposes their entry, Calpurnia puts her down and bridges the racial gap with words worthy of Atticus, though not in his measured idiom, 'It's the same God, ain't it?' (p. 123). The interior of the church is described and, without hymn-books, the congregation follows Zeebo's 'linin'' in concerted song. Then Reverend Sykes preaches against sin, naming the suffering of Tom Robinson's wife, and exacting money from the congregation for her needs. The children contribute, and learn that Helen Robinson is finding it difficult to get work because of the charge against her husband. Calpurnia enlarges upon this, tells Scout to ask Atticus what is meant by rape, and reveals that the congregation 'line' the hymns because they can't read, though she herself taught her son Zeebo. Jem and Scout learn of Calpurnia's 'modest double life' (p. 129), Scout asks if she can visit her in her own home and, when they get back, they find Aunt Alexandra sitting on their porch.

The dramatic and sympathetic force of this chapter is immediate.

The visit to the church extends the children's social, moral and spiritual education, and already the shadows of the Tom Robinson case are gathering. Jem's problems of adolescence, Calpurnia's understanding of them and her handling of Scout's reactions, Scout's own response to Dill's news and her wonderful evaluation of her own growing up and her acknowledgement of relativity – 'I stayed miserable for two days' (p. 120) – provide an ironic flavour to the contrast to come in the visit to the church, the recognition of other richly human standards, the humour of their scrubbed preparations, the poverty in the background and in the immediate foreground as the negroes make sacrifices for one of their own. Visual description of the cemetery indicates deprivation, yet Scout can observe 'It was a happy cemetery' (p. 122). Calpurnia's character is enhanced by her behaviour, her authority, her respect, her humanity – all characteristics she shares with Atticus – but the *revelatory* experience for the children is the main theme of the chapter, with the cheap advertising slogans providing an incongruous contrast with the warm spirituality of the community. The 'linin'' is deep pathos, emphasizing the denial of education to those who are poor *and* black. Calpurnia's instruction of Zeebo from Blackstone's *Commentaries* (the famous and authoritative book on English law) inlays that humour with pathos. The children are also educated into the appreciation, recognition, that Calpurnia has another life away from them, and it is a measure of Scout's maturity and sensitivity that she responds to that knowledge by asking to visit Calpurnia. The chapter ends on a note of climax, for the presence of Alexandra indicates that Atticus is preparing his children for harder times, both without and within, with Calpurnia and Alexandra as the twin supports, though their standards, status and colour are opposed.

Chapter Thirteen (*pp. 130–38*)

Aunt Alexandra announces that she has been invited for a while, and Scout goes over the painfully limited conversations she has had with her in the past. Aunt Alexandra's formidable figure is described, and with the return of Atticus Scout tells the necessary lie that she would like her to stay. Atticus, punning deliberately, says that the summer is going to be a 'hot' one; Aunt Alexandra settles in naturally and gossips, asserts the superiority of the Finch clan, and divides people according to their particular 'Streaks' (drinking, gambling, for example) and is preoccupied with 'heredity' (p. 133). Scout outlines the history, or 'heredity', of Maycomb, and accounts for its remaining the same size by its geographical position, describing the caste system within the ingrown town in some detail. Although they see Alexandra very little for the first month, they manage to stand up to her family snobbery very well by pointing out that Cousin Joshua was known to be insane. Atticus tries to impress upon the children their aunt's view of their 'gentle breeding'; the children feel isolated from this 'new' father, but Scout buries her head in Atticus's vest front, realizes that he has come back to them and that he has no time for Aunt Alexandra's snobbery and false family pride.

This is one of the funniest chapters in the novel. Scout's active mind finds Aunt Alexandra 'irritable on the Lord's Day. I guess it was her Sunday corset' (p. 131); her satirical observations embrace Alexandra's 'What Is Best For The Family' (p. 132) and 'she had river-boat, boarding-school manners' and 'she was born in the objective case' (p. 133) as well as the various 'Streaks', answered in Atticus's imperishable parody, 'Would you say the Finches have an Incestuous Streak?' (p. 133). Jem's canny analogy between the Finches and Ewells is also funny (the more so in view of the exposure of the Ewells to come), and Scout's historical résumé of the Sinkfield activities is both racy and witty. There is also some fine description of Maycomb as it was, set in 'a patchwork sea of cotton fields and timber land' (p. 134). The vein of humour continues in the commonplaces by which people define their local families ('Every Third Merriweather Is Morbid', p. 135), the superb send-up of family snobbery in the account of Cousin Joshua's lunacy, and the fine antithetical positioning of Atticus's remarks on the children's 'gentle breeding' as Scout tries to locate an 'elusive redbug' on her leg (p. 137). There is genuine poignancy in Scout's realization that Atticus does not really subscribe to the breeding theory, balanced by his own joke, 'Get more like

Cousin Joshua every day, don't I?' (p. 138). The lightness of touch throughout this chapter contrasts tellingly with the serious events to come.

Chapter Fourteen (*pp. 138–47*)

The children are aware of a growing anti-Finch atmosphere in the town, but when Scout asks Atticus about rape he learns that she has been to church with Calpurnia and wants to visit her. This leads to a row between Atticus and Aunt Alexandra, in which Scout overhears (she does quite a bit of overhearing in the novel) Atticus assert how much he and the children owe to Calpurnia. He refuses to get rid of her. Jem later lectures Scout on her behaviour to 'Aunty', and they have a fight; they make it up afterwards in unity against Aunt Alexandra, and then dramatically discover Dill hiding under the bed. He has stolen money from his mother's purse, has got to Maycomb by a variety of means, and is now ravenously hungry. Atticus appears, orders them to feed Dill, goes off to get Aunt Rachel, who berates Dill verbally but hugs him in the end. Later that night Dill joins Scout innocently in her bed; he tells her his story, of how his parents buy things for him but don't really want him, and suggests that they get a baby, for he has heard of people from whom you can get them.

This stresses the opposition between Calpurnia and Aunt Alexandra, with the latter's intolerance in part family, in part racial in origin. Scout sees accurately 'the starched walls of a pink cotton penitentiary closing in on me' (p. 140). She overhears Atticus's tribute to Calpurnia, a moving testimony to her father's humanity, and the new tension injected into their family life by Aunt Alexandra is admirably reflected in the fight between Scout and Jem. Even here the humour is present when Scout refers to him as 'You damn morphodite' (p. 141). The drama of the chapter lies in the discovery of Dill, with graphic narration when Dill explains the details of his journey. Atticus's tolerance is obvious again in his attitude to Dill, the pathos of Dill's situation at home and in his seeking out this,

his only home, is stressed and stressed again when he crawls into Scout's bed and talks of getting a baby; this, with its moving fantasies and even more moving innocence, is imbued with the humanity and concern of the author, that richness of compassion which runs throughout the novel and here embraces the two children, who are themselves about to experience adult lack of compassion *or* humanity *or* honesty *or* justice in the sentencing of Tom Robinson.

Chapter Fifteen (*pp. 148–59*)

There follows a week of peace, then nightmare, to use Scout's language. One evening men arrive outside the Finch home. Tom Robinson is to be lodged overnight in Maycomb, and trouble seems imminent. Atticus reaffirms his determination to defend Robinson 'till the truth's told' (p. 149) and remains cool, though Jem is worried, and confides to Scout that he feels someone will hurt Atticus. Tom Robinson is moved to the jail, and on the Sunday evening Atticus goes out, later followed by the children, both concerned on his behalf. They are joined by Dill, and eventually find Atticus sitting outside the jailhouse door. They prepare to go home, but four dusty cars draw up. The men are determined to take Tom Robinson, but Scout bursts into the middle of them, to the horror of Atticus. He orders Jem to go home with Scout, but Jem remains standing there until he is grabbed by one of the men, who is in turn kicked by Scout. She approaches Mr Cunningham, Walter's father, talks about his entailments and about Walter; eventually Mr Cunningham responds to her, says he will say 'hey' to Walter from her, and leads the lynch mob away. All the time Mr Underwood has had them covered from the *Maycomb Tribune* office with his double-barrelled shotgun. Dill carries Atticus's chair home.

The first crowd of men appear from apprehension of trouble, the second with the intention of lynching Tom Robinson. The mood of the chapter is one of racial tension, prejudice, dramatic confrontation, with the theme of developing humanity as seen in Scout's influence on Mr Cunningham, which turns an ugly situation into a retreat from murder. The atmosphere throughout is one of tension. Atticus is revealed as brave and just, his fear only showing when he feels that his children will be involved. His personal integrity never wavers. Jem is inclined to panic (hence his crying out about the telephone ringing), there is an interesting reference to the Ku Klux Klan, which emphasizes the wider history of racial prejudice and persecution and shows that it has not died. Atticus's irony at the 'polite fiction' (p. 150) is motivated by his fear that Tom Robinson will have to pay with his life for what he did not do, while the portrait of Mr Underwood and his practices (p. 151) is very funny, and anticipates his silent protection of Atticus later in the chapter. There is a fine description of Maycomb at night, and a brilliantly incisive and visual one of the jail. It is 'a miniature Gothic joke' (p. 154), its architecture as ugly and dated as the prejudiced view of so many of Maycomb's inhabitants. Some of these, smelling of 'stale whisky and pig-pen' (p. 155), arrive threateningly, but the focus on Jem and Atticus is tellingly revealing of character – like father, like son – in determination and obstinacy. Scout's talking to Mr Cunningham has a kind of running hysterical overtone which reflects her anxiety, and his taking hold of her by both shoulders and telling the men to clear out is symbolic of what Miss Maudie calls the 'first baby-step' – the indication that humanity will win over prejudice in the end. The presence of Mr Underwood and his shotgun again is anticipatory, for he is, so to speak, to fire it later in his verbal condemnation of Tom Robinson's killing. There are unobtrusive symbolic touches too, like Dill's carrying the chair for Atticus (a mark of respect, and a pathetic demonstration of his own need for a father), and in Atticus's massaging of Jem's hair, a 'gesture of affection' (p. 159) which movingly corresponds to Boo Radley's at the bedside of the injured boy he has saved at the end of the novel.

Chapter Sixteen (*pp. 159–69*)

Scout suffers a reaction from the events of the evening, but at breakfast the next morning questions Atticus about Mr Cunningham. Jem joins in, and Atticus forcibly points out that a mob is made up of people, and that a gang was stopped by a child 'because they're still human' (p. 161). Dill comes in with his predictable exaggeration of the night's events, and then they watch people passing by all morning, Dill giving their supposed histories, and Miss Maudie engaging in repartee with a group of 'foot-washers' (p. 163). The children go down to the court in the afternoon, and the 'Roman carnival' (p. 163), which Miss Maudie described, is already beginning outside the courthouse, with the races separated. Mr Dolphus Raymond, who lives with a coloured woman, is described, and his kindness to his children is stressed. Then it is time to go in, and Scout gives an account of the courthouse and its history, and is particularly satirical about the 'Idlers' Club', 'a group of white-shirted, khaki-trousered, suspendered old men' (p. 166). Thanks to the Reverend Sykes the children get seats on the balcony with the negroes, some of the latter yielding up their own. The chapter ends with a visual look at Judge Taylor and his idiosyncrasies.

Scout's reaction associates the events with Atticus and his killing of the mad dog (a wonderfully subconscious analogy, and appropriate too in view of the 'madness' of the mob), and Atticus's 'digging in' (p. 160) against Aunt Alexandra's hostility to Calpurnia shows his tension. His humour never deserts him ('maybe we need a police force of children', p. 161) and his main creed is superbly evoked in 'you children last night made Walter Cunningham stand in my shoes for a minute' (p. 161). There is humour in the account of Mr X. Billups, and even more in Miss Maudie's taking on the foot-washers, her exposure of Miss Stephanie, and the vivid evocation of scene and atmosphere as the various groups wait for the court to open. The story of Mr Dolphus is pathetic and underlines the racial divisions. It also furthers the social and moral education of the children. Scout's description of the courthouse is as positive as her description of the jail, and she concludes that its incongruities reflect 'a people deter-mined to preserve every physical scrap of the past' (p. 166) – and by extension that means maintaining the ascendancy of whites over blacks. The appraisal of the Idlers' Club is superb satire, yet pathetic too in that the old men's knowledge of law and words has become a substitute for living. Scout's learning that Atticus 'aimed to defend him' (Tom Robinson) (p. 167) consciously increases her knowledge of her father's integrity, while the divisions between black and white – the inequalities between man and man – are reflected in the divisions in the court seating. The fact that the children find themselves sitting with the blacks, whose behaviour and courtesy contrasts with that of the whites, is a considered commentary on their loyalty to Atticus *and* a subconscious indication of where their sympathies lie. Judge Taylor, though drawn vividly, is not mere caricature, but he is used to mock the law as well as having an individual astringency of utterance and judgement, as we see from his 'Champertous contrivance' decision, for this means that if he had found in favour of one side, the other would have shared in the damages or money gained.

Chapter Seventeen (*pp. 169–82*)

The first of the three consecutive trial scenes opens with the testimony of Heck Tate; he recalls how he was summoned by Bob Ewell to his house one night because 'some nigger'd raped his girl' (p. 170) and how as a result he arrested Tom Robinson. Atticus asks him if a doctor was sent for to examine the girl – he answers no – and establishes that it was the right side of her face which was badly bruised, and that there were bruises all round her neck. The spectators find this cross-examination dull, though it is to prove very significant later. Scout feels almost optimistic. Bob Ewell is described, as is his permanent idleness, his home behind 'the town garbage dump' (p. 173) which is a rubbish dump itself of rusted and discarded implements, only redeemed by some 'brilliant red geraniums' (p. 174) thought to belong to Mayella Ewell. Scout's account insists that as they watch the case 'We acquired no dramas from watching our father win or lose' (p. 175), but the drama begins with Bob Ewell's testimony. His description of what he saw angers (in a muffled way) the negroes present, and his language involves Judge Taylor in the frequent use of his gavel. Reverend Sykes feels that Jem should take

Scout home, but the children refuse to budge and Judge Taylor asserts that he won't have the court cleared for the time being. Mr Gilmer continues to question Ewell about what he saw, and Atticus then presses the point about no doctor being called. He establishes that Ewell is left-handed, and therefore by implication could have inflicted the injuries to the right side of his daughter's face. Jem is delighted, Scout not so sure.

The narrative style is simple, direct, colloquial throughout this scene, with a dramatic undertone which accentuates the realism of the exchanges. The failure to call a doctor at the time and the demonstration, subtly done by Atticus, that Ewell is left-handed, are the pivots on which the interactions turn. The implication is that it is only a 'nigger' who is being accused. Scout's response to her father's questioning – 'he could make a rape case as dry as a sermon' (p. 173) – ironically conveys the lull before the storm of Ewell's testimony, and Ewell himself, cocky, dim, prejudiced, aggressive, insensitive, ignorant, is vividly evoked both visually and verbally. His 'home' – everything around the cabin seemed 'like the playground of an insane child' (p. 174) – underlines his deprivation and goes some way to explain his aggression, but there is a pathetic element present, the more so when the geraniums, nature alive against the discarded trappings of human nature, are described. Scout's recollections of the Christmas visit are an important indication of the different standards of whites like the Ewells and the 'neat and snug' (p. 175) cabins of the negroes nearby. In a finely ironic first person interjection to the reader, Scout says 'I can't provide any drama' (p. 175), yet the drama is ever-present in the reader's mind because it is *not sensationalized* but accurately reported. There is a certain comedy, unconscious on his part, in Ewell's reply to questions, and his uncompromising language, 'I seen that black nigger yonder ruttin' on my Mayella' (p. 176), draws a sensitive response from Reverend Sykes on the children's account, a careful pointing up of the contrast in behaviour and sensitivity between black and white. Ewell's prejudice against the blacks is heavily underlined, his reference to the 'nigger-nest' (p. 178) even embarrassing the prosecuting counsel. His inhumanity is shown by his not sending for a doctor – it also of course hints at his guilt

– and his ignorance and complacency by the easy way his left-handedness is revealed, and his complete misunderstanding of the word 'ambidextrous'. One deft point is made unobtrusively; one member of the jury is so interested that he leans 'forward with his hands over the railing' (p. 181), an indication that Miss Maudie's first 'baby-step' towards tolerance and justice is being taken.

Chapter Eighteen (*pp. 182–94*)

This opens with the description of Mayella Ewell, her bursting into tears being an attempt, as Jem puts it, to get the judge feeling sorry for her before she goes through what appears to be a carefully rehearsed statement. Atticus ponders carefully on how to handle her in the light of her expressed fear of him and, of course, with some compassion for her circumstances at home. When he speaks to her, she considers that she is being mocked, and Atticus subtly exposes by his quiet questioning the deprived nature of her home existence, the squalid level of life, the joyless monotony which lies at the back of the pathetic creature before him. It is obvious that her father has beaten her many times, but Atticus concentrates on Tom Robinson's alleged attack on her, and then swiftly brings Tom Robinson to his feet to be identified by Mayella. 'His left arm was fully twelve inches shorter than his right' (p. 189) makes Atticus's point visually and dramatically for all to see. Mayella blusters, but is silent when questioned about the absence of the other children, and when asked directly if it was her father or Tom Robinson who beat her up. Then she bursts out, breaks down, and answers no more; Mr Underwood sees the children, Atticus confers with Mr Gilmer, Jem talks to Dill, and Scout remembers that Atticus considers that Judge Taylor is a good judge. He tells Atticus to call his witness.

Mayella's fears, real and imagined, of Atticus are public cover for her unhappy existence in poverty, monotony, and ill-treatment at the hands of her father. A strong moral point is being made, for she has to act as mother to the children. She has also to live with the guilt of what she has done, revealed in the next chapter, and what she is doing – committing perjury. Atticus exposes what he calls the 'polite fiction of Southern womanhood', but the fact that he has to hurt Mayella hurts him. There is a cunning and deliberate echo of the novel's title when Mayella accuses Atticus of 'mockin'' her, for his is the 'song' of humanity and truth, and the real mockery is the Ewells' false testimony and, indeed, the trial itself, a 'mockery' of justice. The description of the Ewells' poverty and sordid life is imbued with the ever-present realism. The skill of Atticus's cross-examination is climaxed by his asking Tom Robinson to stand up, one of the most dramatic moments in the novel. This is almost balanced by the repetitions of silence as Mayella is asked for the truth. Her final outburst comes when she unconsciously punctures the impolite fiction of Southern womanhood by shouting about 'fine fancy gentlemen' and 'yellow stinkin' cowards' (p. 192). The various reactions in court to the end of the cross-examination are economically captured, but Scout has time to focus humorously on Judge Taylor's cigar before the chapter ends, again on a note of climax, with the calling of Tom Robinson.

Chapter Nineteen (*pp. 194–203*)

The simple and direct interrogation of Tom Robinson by Atticus reveals that he has helped Mayella Ewell a number of times. We also notice that she tended the red flowers (geraniums) referred to earlier. Scout registers Mayella's loneliness, and even draws a parallel between her and Boo Radley, summing up her 'mixed child' position, as Jem calls it. Tom tells clearly what happened, how he was invited in by Mayella to repair a door, and describes the unusual and surprising quiet, explained when Mayella told him that she had sent the children to town to buy ice creams. He says that she hugged him, kissed him, said that 'what her papa do to her don't count' (p. 198) and then Ewell appeared and threatened to kill Mayella. Tom fled – 'if you was a nigger like me, you'd be scared too' (p. 199) – and Mr Link Deas interrupts to give Tom a character testimonial which arouses Judge Taylor's wrath. He expels Link Deas from the court. Mr Gilmer's cross-examination is bent on establishing that Tom Robinson lusted after Mayella – after all, he has a criminal record (technically) – though Tom injures his case with the whites in the court by saying that he was 'sorry' for Mayella. The bullying of Tom Robinson moves Dill to tears and Scout has to take him out of the court. He tells her how sick it has made him, and outside they meet Mr Dolphus Raymond, who defines Dill's sensitivity for him.

The impossibility of Tom Robinson's raping Mayella is spelled out in the first paragraph when his useless hand slips off the table, to the embarrassment of Judge Taylor. The cross-examination of Atticus, and Tom's answers, are crisp and to the point, a reflection of Tom's simple truthfulness, again revelatory of the Ewells' poverty and the pathetic isolation of Mayella. Tom's idiom is realistically and un-sensationally captured in his reportage of what took place, climaxed by Mayella's hugging him; this brings down Judge Taylor's gavel and, dramatically, the court lights come on, a symbolic reflection that the truth has come to light, a finely ironic touch by the author. The major revelation of the chapter almost passes unnoticed in Tom's testimony, which quietly shows that Mayella has been forced by her father – raped might be the appropriate word – sexually on a number of occasions, thus adding another level of irony to the accusation against Tom. Link Deas's interruption is dramatic – it is another 'first baby-step' – and the racial assumptions of Mr Gilmer ensure that in essence Tom is going to be found guilty because he is black and has dared to feel sorry for a pathetically inadequate white girl who in turn dared to break the code, as Atticus is to point out, and kiss a black man. The final section shows what we have always known: that Dill is sensitive and emotional as well as imaginative, and Scout's 'after all he's just a Negro' (p. 203) shows that his humanity is in advance of hers, which has been conditioned by the traditional divisions of Maycomb and the South.

Chapter Twenty (*pp. 204–10*)

Mr Dolphus Raymond comforts Dill with Coca-Cola, thus belying his own reputation as a drinking man; he has established the myth,

since that is what people want to believe of a man who has broken
the code and merely wants to live his own life. He spells out 'the
hell white people give coloured folks' (p. 205) and tells Scout how
different her own father is. They get back into court for Atticus's
final address to the jury; to the children's dismay he loosens his clothes,
something they have never seen him do before. His summary is simply
put: 'This case is as simple as black and white' (p. 207) and he spells
out the fact that Mayella has broken the severe code of her society
by tempting a black man, kissing him, and then trying to destroy
the 'evidence of her offence' (p. 208) by ensuring that the man was
charged with raping her. Atticus sweats as he warms to his case, and
quotes the wider context of Thomas Jefferson's 'all men are created
equal' (p. 209) before applying it to the courts of justice of the land,
for all men are equal before the law. His final plea is for the jury
to do their duty, though Jem thinks he adds 'In the name of God,
believe him' (p. 210). At this critical juncture Calpurnia appears and
walks up the central aisle towards Atticus.

The whole of this chapter must be studied in detail, for it is the
central focus of the novel in dramatic, moving, humanitarian intensity
and involvement. It is deftly balanced – we move from Mr Dolphus
Raymond's particular case to the climax of the vitally particular case
– that of a man on trial for his life. Everything that Atticus says is
redolent of humanity, compassion, justice, having a universality that
goes beyond the courtroom and into the prejudices and inhumanities
of the world outside; the reasoning and the evidence show that Tom
Robinson is not guilty, and in elevating the principle of justice and
the responsibilities of the courts and juries Atticus is ironically asking
the jury to find themselves *guilty* – if they so judge Tom Robinson
– or *not guilty* – if they find him so. Atticus's loosening of his clothes
is yet another master-stroke by the author: it is a symbolic *freeing*
of himself from what surrounds him, so that his mind will transcend
the petty prejudice, the society blackmail of which he is so acutely
aware. The clarity of the style in this chapter is remarkable; there
is nothing in Atticus's speech which sounds a false note, no departure
from his dedication to the truth. The entrance of Calpurnia is anti-
climax after that speech, but climax for the children, who suspect

she has come in search of them; it is an effective, down-to-earth contrast.

Chapter Twenty-One (*pp. 210–16*)

The children descend from the coloured balcony, and Atticus, exhausted, relents and allows them to stay. They go home while the jury are out, Jem misguidedly exultant because he thinks they are going to win. When they return to the court Jem has a discussion with Reverend Sykes, and then there is the long wait for the jury's return. Scout dreams, but then gets the uncomfortable feeling of the cold February morning when her father shot the dog in the deserted street, and 'the mockingbirds were still' (p. 214). The jury do not look at Tom Robinson; they find him guilty. As Atticus passes from the court all the negroes stand in respect.

The brief interlude at home has all the tension and excitement generated by the court battle, with Calpurnia's and Aunt Alexandra's reactions equally predictable, while Jem's confidence and Scout's exhilaration, both transient, reflect the hard nature of education in life. The stillness of the courtroom is wonderfully conveyed as they wait for the verdict, the negroes with 'biblical patience' (p. 213). Scout's imagination works at a high pitch, and her shivering and her memories are an anticipation of what she subconsciously fears will come. The reference to that past occasion when 'the mockingbirds were still', the superb contrast between 'a deserted, waiting, empty street, and the court-room was packed with people' (p. 214), the association again with the past as the jury move like underwater swimmers (see p. 32 of these notes) and the intuition conveyed by 'watching all the time knowing that the gun was empty' (p. 215), all these convey the child's imaginative response to crisis. And perhaps the most moving moment in the whole novel is conveyed by the negroes' silent homage to the man who has taken more than a 'baby-step' on their behalf.

Chapter Twenty-Two (*pp. 216–21*)

The aftermath of the verdict is moving, with Jem upset at the injustice, Aunt Alexandra conveying sympathy by calling Atticus 'brother', and the negro community piling gifts on Atticus and his family, despite the hard times in which they live. Atticus is greatly touched, and Dill arrives to report his aunt's reaction. The gossip begins again, led of course by Miss Stephanie, who questions the children, but she is headed off by Miss Maudie, who has shown her sympathy by making them some cakes. She is their principal solace too, telling them that Judge Taylor had his motive for nominating Atticus to take the case. She points out that only Atticus could have caused the jury to keep out so long, and tells them that 'we're making a step – it's just a baby-step, but it's a step' (p. 220). Dill's reaction is that he will be a clown when he grows up, and Miss Stephanie delightedly reports the news that Bob Ewell has spat in Atticus's face and threatened to kill him.

This short chapter effectively reports the reactions – the sorrow and anger, differently conveyed, of Jem and Dill, Atticus's acid comparison of his children being at the trial as 'as much Maycomb County as missionary teas' (p. 216) and his moving 'seems that only children weep' (p. 217) over man's injustice and prejudice against man. Dill's own identification is seen in his impatience with his aunt and his wish to be a clown; Jem's 'feral' noise conveys his opinion of the gossips, Miss Stephanie's repeated questions, her joy at having more gossip fodder provided for her. Miss Maudie, close in idealism and practice to Atticus in every way, redresses the moral balance and also indicates that *others* are taking the 'baby-step', such as Judge Taylor. Again the chapter ends on a note of climax, with the threat to Atticus, thus building the tension which characterizes the rest of the novel.

Chapter Twenty-Three (*pp. 221–31*)

Atticus's calm reaction to the incident, which even Miss Stephanie acknowledges is 'right dry' (p. 211), is contrasted with the fear of his children on his account. He urges them to stand in Bob Ewell's shoes for a minute, but even Aunt Alexandra is fearful. Jem is for the abolition of juries, and during their discussion Atticus refers to the white man who cheats a black man as 'trash' (p. 225). He also reveals that one member of the jury, a Cunningham, was originally for the acquittal of Tom Robinson, another indication of the 'baby-step'. Scout is for seeking out Walter Cunningham later and inviting him back to dinner, but Aunt Alexandra's caste system finds her rigidly opposed to the suggestion. Jem leads the angry Scout away from this, shows her the first hair on his chest and under his arms (which she can't see). He also lectures her on the various kinds of people, but Scout comes to the conclusion, which Atticus would surely applaud, that 'there's just one kind of folks. Folks' (p. 231).

Atticus's invitation to Jem to try and stand in Bob Ewell's shoes indicates his wide tolerance and humanity – themes given structural coherence and solidity after the trial – for he fears for the Ewell family's sufferings at their father's hands. In discussion with Jem his 'the white man always wins' (p. 224) shows his recognition of the inadequacy of the law to redress racial prejudice, but his use of the word 'trash' to describe the cheating white man reveals the depth of his passion, which is usually kept well under control. He sounds a prophetic note when he accepts that one day white society will have to pay for its prejudice, and this is underlined by the fact that women cannot serve on juries in Alabama. Atticus's astuteness in not object-ing to a Cunningham on the jury is demonstrated, and his wisdom is shown in Jem's repeating his remark that you can choose your friends but not your family. Alexandra's picking up of Atticus's word 'trash' to describe Walter Cunningham is authorial irony, since Alexandra is debasing the use by her snobbery. Jem's immaturity (over his hair) and his growing maturity of mind when he discusses people are shown, and Scout's equation of negroes with Englishmen is a delightfully humorous touch which her father would have appreciated. Jem has the last word. His insights and sensitivity are developing fast; he begins to understand why Boo Radley doesn't come out. In terms of the structure of the novel this realization is deftly placed; when Boo does come out (Chapter Twenty-Eight) it is in order to save Jem's life.

Chapter Twenty-Four (*pp. 231–42*)

This chapter describes the meeting of the missionary circle in the Finch household; Scout has been dressed with conformist femininity for the occasion. She carries in the coffee pitcher, and reveals that she is wearing her 'britches' under her dress. Asked if she is going to be a lawyer when she grows up, she replies that she is going to be a lady. The ladies present talk about Tom Robinson's wife and children; their tone conveys that the negroes, upset of course by the trial, are largely ineducable, the ladies exclaiming at their inability to make Christians of them! Their innuendo is directed at those people in the town, like Atticus, who thought that they were doing right. Miss Maudie counteracts this tone by the individuality of her own, but Mrs Merriweather continues her harangue, indicting the Northerners for pretending to make the negroes their equals. Atticus enters dramatically, takes Alexandra, Maudie and Scout into the kitchen, and tells them the news that Tom Robinson has been shot dead while trying to escape. While Cal and Atticus go to comfort Mrs Robinson, and Alexandra breaks down, feeling that her brother is being torn apart by his involvement in the case, Miss Maudie pulls them together and they rejoin the ladies, Scout playing her new role to perfection by offering a tray of cookies to Mrs Merriweather.

This is a brilliantly satirical chapter, contrasting with the two which preceded it, and heightened by the dramatic news brought by Atticus which sufficiently indicates his distance from these ostentatious do-gooders meeting in his house, perhaps the most truly Christian house in the town. Scout's humorous comments balance the earthy realities of the lifestyle of the Mrunas with the lifestyle of these ladies who think they are fighting 'the good fight' (p. 232) although they are protected from such realities. The emphasis on food carries its own moral comment, while the virtual uniformity of dress and make-up calls forth Scout's irony; there is a fine moment of self-humour when she reveals that she is wearing her 'britches' under her feminine dress. The sympathetic support of Miss Maudie sustains Scout through Miss Stephanie's inquisition, but Scout herself closely scrutinizes Mrs Merriweather's self-indulgence, for that lady's 'large brown eyes always filled with tears when she considered the oppressed' (p. 234). Scout's mild answer that she wants to be a 'lady' is dropped deliberately into a company of women who are trying to be ladies but have only their superficialities to recommend them. The running humour of the scene is also conveyed by the imagery used about Mrs Merriweather ('organ', 'measure', 'chimes'), and by Scout's thinking – or pretending to think – that the ladies are talking of Mayella Ewell when they are speaking of Tom Robinson's wife, and further by Mrs Merriweather complaining about having a 'darky' in the kitchen as they go on eating Calpurnia's food. Mrs Farrow's sibilants also contribute to the comedy, as do 'the soft bovine sounds of the ladies munching their dainties' (p. 237). The wide world is not forgotten, with Mrs Roosevelt taking an adult step towards equality which these ignorant 'ladies' condemn. Before the news of Tom Robinson's death, Scout thinks of how hopeless he felt according to what Atticus had told her, a hopelessness reflected in his almost deranged attempt to escape. The number of times Tom Robinson was shot is also significant, since it represents the uncompromising rule of law by force. Miss Maudie's simple gesture in untying Calpurnia's apron shows her natural humanity and symbolizes perhaps the coming freedom of people like Cal from those they serve. There is further insight into Alexandra's character when she gives way, while Miss Maudie's superb definition of Atticus's integrity – 'We trust him to do right' (p. 240) – and her whole attitude express her own.

Chapter Twenty-Five (*pp. 242–5*)

Jem orders Scout to put a roly-poly outside, instead of killing it. He tells Scout that roly-polies don't hurt anybody, and later she recalls what Dill had told her about the visit to Helen Robinson, Atticus having picked Jem and Dill up on the way when he met them. Atticus is kind to one of the children, but Dill describes how Helen just fell down in the dirt without Atticus having to tell her that her husband was dead. Local interest lasts for two days, but Mr Underwood, of the *Maycomb Tribune*, speaks out – 'He likened Tom's death to the senseless slaughter of songbirds by hunters and children' (p. 245). Bob Ewell's sworn revenge still lurks in Scout's mind.

There is a strong humanitarian focus in this chapter, with Jem's increasing humanity (the roly-poly is as innocent as a mockingbird or Tom Robinson), Dill's graphic account of the visit to Helen Robinson, and Scout's deepening realization of what the law cannot do: 'Atticus had used every tool available to free men to save Tom Robinson, but in the secret courts of men's hearts Atticus had no case' (p. 245).

Chapter Twenty-Six (*pp. 245–51*)

The resumption of school, with Scout once more becoming interested in the Radley place; she remembers the incidents of the past, and invents a fantasy about Arthur Radley. Atticus warns her not to start this up again, and the events of the summer continue to hang over the family. Scout describes the Current Events periods in school, including one in which they discuss Hitler and the Jews, and Miss Gates, the teacher, defines democracy with a little help from Scout, who later discusses the question of Hitler with Atticus, and points out that Miss Gates, who has condemned persecution in the class discussion, actually said (of the negroes after the trial) 'it's time somebody taught 'em a lesson' (p. 251).

Scout's sensitivity is revealed in her 'twinge of remorse' (p. 246) over the past torment of Arthur Radley, and her imagination in her fantasy meeting with Mr Arthur, a meeting which is to come true, unexpectedly and dangerously, in the near future. Again we note the tight structure of the novel. There is the usual unobtrusive but effective imagery ('the summer hung over us like smoke in a closed room', p. 247) and the usual satire of limited educational practice, here the short talk delivered by a member of the class. The divisions between town and country children – the latter having few if any newspapers – are emphasized, but the main satirical and ironic weighting of the chapter is on Miss Gates's indictment of prejudice, her praise of democracy, her appraisal of the wider context – a nation breeding hate and injustice – blinding her to the local one – white hating and persecuting black. There is a keen insight into Jem's anguish at the end of the chapter in his wish to gain weight and be a footballer, and his not wanting the courthouse mentioned. He has hardly yet understood how his feelings have been educated.

Chapter Twenty-Seven (*pp. 251–8*)

Bob Ewell loses his job with the WPA, and Judge Taylor hears a scratching noise at the back of his house; he sits watchfully with a shotgun across his lap. Helen Robinson, employed by Link Deas, walks out of her way to work for him in order to avoid the Ewells, but Link Deas threatens Bob Ewell. There follows the account of Miss Tutti and Miss Frutti Barber, whose furniture is stolen and hidden in their own cellar by children, Scout laconically observing, 'I deny having taken part in such a thing' (p. 256). Scout is cast as a ham in Mrs Merriweather's Halloween pageant depicting the agricultural products of Maycomb County, but Atticus and Alexandra both get out of seeing it, leaving Jem to conduct Scout.

The joke played on Miss Tutti and Miss Frutti balances the fears about Bob Ewell, perhaps manifested in his following Helen Robinson, and the comedy of the Maycomb pageant imparts a false lightness to the narrative (perhaps as false as the pageant itself), so that we are aware of a lessening of tension, a stay before the crisis (there have been sufficient hints that one is to come), rather like the delay occasioned by the porter's scene in *Macbeth* before Duncan's murder is discovered. The appropriateness of Scout's being cast as a ham is emphasized by her later performance, while the satirical comment on Mrs Merriweather's 'Maycomb County, Maycomb County, we will aye be true to thee' is not only a small-town patriotism cloyingly derivative of the national one but is, of course, for whites only. The incident with Judge Taylor, Aunt Alexandra finishing what she had to say in mid-sentence, and the end of the chapter when Scout says 'Thus began our longest journey together' are all ominous forecasts of the danger to come.

Chapter Twenty-Eight (*pp. 258–70*)

Jem escorts Scout to the pageant and they joke about ghosts while 'a solitary mocker poured out his repertoire' (p. 259) above them. Scout trips, gets up, and Cecil Jacobs jumps out in front of them to scare them. Scout goes with Cecil (spending their 'first nickels on the House of Horrors', p. 260) and visits other booths before she gets backstage to find her costume 'mashed' (p. 261). Mrs Merriweather announces her pageant, translating its Latin title inaccurately, and then proceeds to a commentary which has the effect of causing Scout to fall asleep and only wake for the finale, when she makes her entrance to the distress of Mrs Merriweather and the delight of Judge Taylor. Offered a lift home, the children refuse it, and, impeded by Scout's costume which is enclosed with chicken wire, set off. They are being followed, and sense that it is Cecil Jacobs, but when Scout calls him a big fat hen there is no response. Scout cannot remove her costume, though Jem has her dress, since she has nothing on underneath. They stop near the big oak, are suddenly attacked, but someone pulls Scout's attacker off; she finds a man smelling of whisky on the ground, and then sees another man carrying the injured Jem towards their house; she gets there herself, is met by Atticus and Alexandra, and Doctor Reynolds is sent for. Then Alexandra frees her from the chicken wire, but Scout is all anxiety for Jem, sees him (he has been sedated, and has a broken arm) and notices a man she doesn't know leaning against the wall in the room. Then Heck Tate comes in to announce that he has found Scout's dress, and that Bob Ewell is lying dead under the tree with a kitchen knife stuck into his ribs.

This is the finest chapter of the novel in terms of sheer narrative drama. Once again the mockingbird image is used with telling irony. Here it applies not only to the innocence of the bird (and the children) but to the 'mocking' of truth and justice by the 'solitary' Bob Ewell. There is a fine contrast between the darkness the children go through, symbolic of the darkness of the evil in Bob Ewell's heart against his daughter and the children, and the lights of the auditorium, lights of safety but at the same time false lights of 'white' status and tradition. Cecil Jacobs in mock attack is a brilliant forecasting parody of the attack to come, as is the visit to the House of Horrors, a 'mocking' of the genuine horror which the children are shortly to experience. There are fine touches of humour (the whole of Mrs Merriweather's pageant, as garrulous and irrelevant as a missionary tea) and irony in the children refusing a lift home. The tense atmosphere is maintained there and back – the hot night, the fact that it is Halloween, the 'stillness before a thunderstorm' (p. 264), the echo of Scout's 'big fat hen' shout, the suddenness of the attack, the superb economy of the narrative conveying the speed with which everything has happened. Short, staccato sentences reflect the breathing, the reactions, the tense dialogue, the ponderous but sure movements of Heck Tate and his own studied relaying of his important news are in longer, more leisurely sentences as he exudes an atmosphere of calm after the crisis. The narrative drama within the chapter is graphic; Tate's revelation of Ewell's death at the end is a subtly achieved climax, with a sense of mystery conveyed by the as yet unidentified man standing in the room.

Chapter Twenty-Nine (*pp. 271–4*)

In reaction Scout notices that Atticus's age is beginning to show, and Aunt Alexandra leaves the room, blaming herself because she had a feeling that something was going to happen that night. Her head in Atticus's lap, Scout describes what she heard and saw; Atticus and the neighbours had their radios on at the time, and heard nothing. Tate reveals that Ewell had puncture marks on his arms, which must have come from the wire of Scout's costume, which he had tried to cut. The costume had saved Scout's life, but so had the man in the room. Scout points to him, describes his appearance, and is moved to tears when she realizes that it is Boo Radley. He has effectively come out when needed.

The descriptions of Atticus and Aunt Alexandra reflect the strain they have been under, but Heck Tate gets on with the questioning and elucidates everything by the directness of his approach; consequently the dialogue is crisp, economical, with some humour as Tate tries to grasp the fact that Scout was a 'ham'. Easily the most significant part of the chapter is the description of Boo Radley, and in particular the account of his 'whiteness'. The reiteration of his colour has a symbolic force, for in the darkness of the setting his whiteness is seen as a giving to others – he risks himself – just as Tom Robinson, a black, gave his time and help to Mayella Ewell in her loneliness. White and black are therefore one – humanity transcends the colour of the skin – and the chapter once more ends on a moving note of climax.

Chapter Thirty (*pp. 275–81*)

Atticus gently corrects Scout, and introduces her to Mr Arthur Radley, the Boo of the children's fantasies. With the return of Dr Reynolds, Atticus goes out to discuss things with Heck Tate, having convinced himself that Jem has killed Bob Ewell. Scout tactfully leads Arthur away to a chair in the dark, where he will be 'more comfortable'. Heck Tate puts Atticus right – Atticus's principles will not allow him to have any cover-up over his son – asserting that Bob Ewell killed himself. Heck himself is intent on another cover-up, for he wants to save Arthur Radley (who did kill Ewell) from the glare of publicity he would have to face for coming out. Atticus at last understands what Heck is trying to do, for he has even removed the knife that Ewell was carrying, explaining, truthfully, that he 'took it off a drunk man' (p. 274) (though omitting to say that the drunk man is dead). Heck takes full responsibility – 'it is my decision' (p. 274) – and virtually challenges Atticus to take him on if he wishes. The explanation Atticus tells Scout is that Ewell fell on his knife, and Scout responds by supporting Heck's account after he has left.

There is wonderful duality about this chapter, the 'curious contrast' between Heck and Atticus, the one engineering, the other opposing, a cover-up; yet there is a sameness too, for Heck is motivated by the humanitarian concern he has seen in Atticus. We are taken in memory back to the beginning of the novel when Atticus said 'Sometimes it's better to bend the law a little in special cases' (p. 36), for here the law of humanity is made to bend the facts. The 'baby-step' has become a large one, for Heck is repaying Atticus's humanity, summarizing it as 'There's a black boy dead for no reason, and the man responsible for it's dead ... Let the dead bury the dead' (p. 280). Scout invokes the central symbol of the novel, saying that to bring Arthur to trial would be 'sort of like shootin' a mockingbird' (p. 280). The words carry the poignancy of her fuller understanding, while Atticus's 'Thank you for my children, Arthur' (p. 281) carry the fullness of his. Arthur will live on in his silent song, and Scout and Jem will never again mock this mockingbird.

Chapter Thirty-One (*pp. 281–5*)

Arthur and his terrible cough are described more fully, and then Scout leads him to Jem's bedside. He is curious and uncertain, but Scout urges him to touch Jem, and then takes him home. When she turns to leave, she realizes that she is seeing the neighbourhood from a new angle, and the night fades in her memory. She views all the events she has recounted from this new perspective, Boo's perspective, watching *his* children – Jem and Scout – through the seasons of the years, as she stands in his shoes. She thinks what she'll tell Jem the next day, and gets home to find Atticus appropriately reading *The Grey*

Ghost. Scout dozes against Atticus, but he carries her to bed while she tells him of incidents in the book, blurring the memories of them with Boo Radley, while Atticus goes to spend the night at Jem's bedside.

Arthur's touching of Jem is a kind of blessing, and Scout learns 'his body English'. When he asks to be taken home it is 'in the voice of a child afraid of the dark' (p. 282), a wonderfully effective way of emphasizing that he is a 'child' and consequently stressing his courage in venturing out to save the children. Scout's own humanity is indicated when she says that she never saw Arthur again, and that she and her family have never given him anything (the corollary, sensitively unvoiced, is that merely by seeing them, observing them, he has been given a family, reinforced by Scout's reference to herself and Jem as 'Boo's children'). The retrospect from the Radley porch is poetic, and endorses Atticus's main tenet of belief, that you have to be in someone else's shoes and walk around in them if you are to appreciate their viewpoint. Scout shows marvellous resilience in wanting to listen to the 'scary' story *The Grey Ghost* and, by a subtle sleight of hand, the author merges the events of the story and the events of the evening in Scout's drowsy recollections. Atticus's care for her, his night vigil with Jem, show the practical and emotional sympathy of the man who serves a wider cause but whose private and public life have been governed by the same principles.

Characters

ATTICUS

Harper Lee's choice of name for the most important character in her novel refers us to the Atticus of Roman history: Titus Pomponius (109–32 B.C.), the friend and correspondent of Cicero. According to the *Oxford Classical Dictionary*, his 'calculating policy of neutrality is hard to justify'.

The Atticus of the novel, however, is neutral in a positive sense, and his neutrality – the impartiality of enlightened and humanitarian views – is easy to justify. Atticus's tolerance transcends the prejudice around him. He has a certain child-like quality ('Lawyers, I suppose, were children once', says Charles Lamb's epigraph to the novel). It is as if he has grown up in experience but returned to the innocence of simple and basic morality. Atticus is also a wise man. When he is reported as saying 'Our father said we were both right', it is not the cowardice of compromise but the wisdom of perspective. It is these qualities, then: humanity, the impartiality which allows him to see all sides of a problem, his strong, innocent morality and his warmth which the children learn to admire as they grow up. As they learn to appreciate them, so do we. Like Scout and Jem, we come to see them as absolutely necessary to a fully human life. Let us examine them in more detail.

Although Atticus has a dislike for the practice of criminal law, he makes a reasonable income from it in Maycomb, and is 'satisfactory' – in reality a term of high praise – to his children, whom he treats 'with courteous detachment'. Atticus is considerate and sympathetic, keeping his counsel about the Radleys, for example. He is generous in spirit and warm, as he demonstrates when he refers to Mrs Dubose as the bravest person he ever knew. He always has time for his children, but lets them develop their ideas and attitudes freely from their experience. He watches over and guides Jem, while Scout always finds his lap available when she needs love, reassurance and understanding. Atticus is a quiet but sound judge of human nature, knowing that when he helps Mr Cunningham, the latter, who hasn't ready money, will pay him in some form, and there is no complacency or greed in his attitude. His consideration for others – elevated to moral responsibility – is shown when he puts young Walter Cunningham at ease by talking about crops and by deliberately not noticing the boy pouring syrup over his vegetables. His wide enlightenment is shown in his employing the negress Calpurnia, though 'employing' is here used only in a technical sense, for Calpurnia is one of the family, the surrogate mother to Jem and Scout, and she is never treated by Atticus as a servant.

Atticus's humanitarian creed is summed up in his phrase that you cannot understand anyone 'until you climb into his skin and walk around in it' and this creed is fundamental to the moral education of his children, with Jem suffering in Mrs Dubose's skin and Scout finding understanding in Boo Radley's. Atticus follows his own creed with unobtrusive resolution and without arrogance. His compassion is everywhere apparent, for instance his tolerance of the Ewells' shooting out of season springs from his awareness of the 'hunger pains' of the Ewell children. His compromise with Scout over school and reading shows him as a domestic diplomat, activated by sympathy.

Atticus has a wonderful sense of humour, sometimes expressed in the legalistic phrases he uses. Thus his appraisal of the children's 'morphodite' finds them guilty of 'near libel'. When Boo Radley has placed the blanket around Scout, Atticus, knowing of his children's fantasies about the Radleys, ironically says 'Do not let this inspire you to further glory, Jeremy', a subtle recall of Jem's previous 'glory' when he had lost his pants in the Radley garden. Perhaps best of all is his mocking (note the word) of Alexandra's caste theory, when he asks, 'Would you say the Finches have an Incestuous Streak?' He is practical and sympathetic when Miss Maudie's house catches fire, and so relaxed that he seems to be watching a football game. This contrasts very effectively with his shooting of the mad dog Tim Johnson, for here we see another side of Atticus's character, a kind of humility. He has to be urged by Heck Tate to revert to his past for a moment – the fame of 'one-shot Finch' – and the loss of his glasses is a masterstroke, for they symbolize his present, a present in which he has renounced his great skill as a marksman, feeling, as Miss Maudie puts it, that God 'had given him an unfair advantage'. He realizes immediately that this new image of himself presented to his children may give them a wrong sense of perspective, and redresses the balance later by praising what he calls real courage in the form of Mrs Dubose's fight to die 'free' from her addiction.

Atticus has pride – not the false pride of family status – but pride allied to integrity, which makes him accept the brief to defend Tom Robinson. He knows he can't win, and that he would never again be able to hold up his head in town or get his children to 'mind' him if he didn't fight this fight, even though he knows it means 'fighting our friends'. His sense of duty is exemplified here, and in minor key that sense of duty is shown in his insistence on visiting his sister every Christmas.

Atticus has a courtroom voice, a kindly domestic voice, a stern voice, as well as what Scout expressively calls 'last-will-and-testament diction'. And just as he has to persuade in court, so he has to persuade in life. Giving the children air-rifles is a fine example of this, for one-shot Finch, who has learned humanity and will only shoot from compassion, gives his children the opportunity to learn in the same way. Here, as elsewhere, he displays an astuteness close to cunning. Consider him telling Uncle Jack exactly what is involved in the Tom Robinson case, knowing all the time that Scout is listening. In this way she will learn of his dedication to the fight against racial prejudice, and if he is devious here it is from the highest possible motive – the education of his children into humane standards of judgement regardless of colour, class or creed. At the trial he loses the battle against Southern prejudice, but his influence on Mr Cunningham and Heck Tate ensure that the war will finally be won.

Atticus's statement that 'it's a sin to kill a mockingbird' is the key to the essential gentleness of his character. He is 'too old' to play games like the other fathers, yet ironically he takes part in the greatest game of all with the odds stacked against him – the fight for a man's life. For Atticus, the mockingbirds represent innocence, the joy of life and freedom, singing their hearts out for others, and he unswervingly asserts their right to be preserved, like Tom Robinson or Boo Radley. As Miss Maudie says, he is 'civilized in his heart', but he is also civilized in his behaviour – witness his courtesy to Mrs Dubose, which makes Scout think he is 'the bravest man who ever lived', words which echo Atticus's own description of Mrs Dubose's courage. He is indeed courageous himself, knowing that he will lose the Tom Robinson case but seeing it through 'no matter what', driven on by self-respect, duty and compassion. This latter quality stands out, and we note his pity for Mayella Ewell, and the fact that forcing her to reveal that she has broken the code of Southern womanhood by kissing a negro hurts him deeply. Atticus sees not only the fate of Tom Robinson in her perjury, but also the deprivation and loneliness that lie behind it. We must also remember his compassion to Dill when he turns up unexpectedly, and his concern for his children when the potential lynching squad threatens the solitary guard he has mounted on the jail. Here he nearly reaches breaking point, but not out of fear for himself. Scout notices that when he gets up his fingers are trembling and he moves like an old man. This is a revealing insight into the tremulous humanity of the man whose feelings are generally well under control. Later, he leans against the wall of the jail in reaction and relief, and on the way home strokes Jem's head, 'his one gesture of affection'. In reaction he afterwards resorts to his ironic brand of humour, telling Jem that after the previous night's experience with a Southern mob 'maybe we need a police force of children'.

The court scene, that stereotype of fiction and film, is not just a dramatic gimmick in the narrative of *To Kill a Mockingbird*. It translates the private Atticus into the public one, elevating his domestic humanity and exposing his broad, humanitarian views to the glare of publicity which the naturally retiring Atticus would normally shun. This happens not just from choice, but from his own strong beliefs.

Atticus coolly establishes the lack of credibility in the Ewell story by eliciting the fact that no doctor was ever called to examine Mayella Ewell after the alleged rape. Atticus is clever enough to make what he doesn't say as important as what he does say, for there is a running implication throughout that Bob Ewell has forced his daughter sexually and beaten her on many occasions while drunk. The lawyer Atticus – it is his finest hour – demonstrates by common-sense interrogation (and a fine sense of the dramatic) that the withered left arm of Tom Robinson could not have inflicted the injuries to the right side of Mayella's face. He further shows, by getting Bob Ewell to write his name, and so revealing that he too is left-handed, that Ewell almost certainly beat up his daughter for kissing a negro and so breaking the code of Southern womanhood. The symbol of the mockingbird suddenly becomes equated with Atticus himself when Mayella accuses him of 'mocking' her, and Atticus's song of humanity can't alter the fact that the verdict is a mockery also. Atticus's skill builds up a picture of the sordid deprivations of the Ewells' home life, but such is his own capacity to stand in someone else's shoes that when he realizes that he has exposed Mayella, revealed the truth, he is hurt to the core on account of this poor, lonely, degraded and lost girl. Just as he loses his glasses in the urgent need to see clearly and shoot accurately at the mad dog, so in the courtroom he does something the children have never seen him do before: he loosens his clothing, symbolically shedding any inhibitions and at the same time freeing himself from the prejudice around him (perhaps inviting others to free themselves too). His language is the man. He uncompromisingly spells out the truth to those who have no will to hear it and no intention of accepting it: 'This case is as simple as black and white.' From then on his analysis of the pathetic Mayella's motivation is concise, incontrovertible, direct – 'She tempted a negro', 'she kissed a black man' – and he then proceeds to outline the prejudice against negroes and demolish it with the succinct rhetoric of truth. He demonstrates the fallacy of the assertion that all men are created equal, and then, ironically and perhaps bitterly, defines the 'living, working reality' of the court and jury system.

Inevitably Atticus suffers a reaction after the verdict, saying that if he doesn't wake up in the morning he's not to be called. He is deeply moved when the gifts of food are sent to him by the negroes, particularly as times are hard. As usual, Miss Maudie pronounces on Atticus's achievement, saying that he is one of the men who are born to do unpleasant jobs for the rest, and that in this instance he was chosen because a 'step' had to be made. But Atticus soon settles into his less obviously emotional ways, observing after Bob Ewell has spat in his face that he wished that he 'wouldn't chew tobacco' and telling Jem that this has probably saved 'Mayella Ewell one extra beating'. In saying that Ewell has now got his hatred out of his system Atticus is again asserting his faith in human nature. But in this instance his faith is misplaced. For once he takes up an extreme stance, saying that white men who cheat black men are 'trash' and that one day the price of the terrible prejudice will have to be paid. His cleverness is again shown when he reveals that he did not object to having a Cunningham on the jury, for he was subtly calculating on his own and Scout's influence on that family.

Miss Maudie obviously admires Atticus and recognizes that she is paying him a high tribute when she says simply 'We trust him to do right'. He does, he always does, but he is not a cloyingly idealized or sentimentalized figure. Atticus suffers, and we watch him suffer, for what injures man injures him and some of those injuries are self-inflicted. Atticus does not shirk a challenge, or duck a responsibility, nor does he speak vaingloriously. He is naturally kind to Helen Robinson's children, for he has an inherent good breeding which transcends the claims of superior caste made by his sister. His integrity is shown once again when, believing that Jem killed Bob Ewell, he refuses to have it hushed up but – and this is an index to his reality – he is frail enough to accept the hushing up on Arthur Radley's account, Scout's moral comment – 'it'd be sort of like shooting a mockingbird, wouldn't it?' – sufficiently reminding him of his own previously expressed views on that subject. He is finally optimistic after the near tragedy, telling Scout that most people are nice 'when you finally see them' and spending the night in sympathetic silence and responsibility by Jem's bedside. We leave him almost as we first saw him. He is within the domestic circle, kind, considerate, thoughtful, drily witty and ironic. Atticus is a man of principle, integrity, courage. He is dedicated to humanity through the removal of prejudice. His accepting the Tom Robinson case is a 'step' towards justice and it ensures that there will be others like it.

SCOUT

Harper Lee's first-person narrator uses Atticus's own maxim: she steps back into the skin of the young Jean Louise Finch and walks around in it. The whole story is told in retrospect. We see a woman looking back on a particular period of her childhood with a wonderful imaginative intensity. The events are made graphic and immediate as if they were happening at the time, but there is occasional and unobtrusive evaluation of these events by the woman that the child was to become. A contemporary review of the novel (in *The Saturday Review* in 1960) suggested that the method made for inconsistency, but if the reader once accepts that the childhood experiences are informed by hindsight throughout then no inconsistency is possible.

Scout is an intelligent and sensitive girl, something of a tomboy. The novel is about the education of her mind, her feelings, her morality. This happens largely through the enlightenment of her father's attitudes and the warmth of his sympathy. Her mother is dead, and the children have to fend for themselves for much of the day, hence their fantasies and imaginative games. She has both historical and social awareness. She knows the background to her family and then, at a somewhat wider level, she has contact with her various neighbours. She brings the 'tired old town' of Maycomb alive by the quality of her ironic observation, capturing Miss Stephanie, Miss Maudie, Mr Avery, Mr Dolphus Raymond and Judge Taylor in vivid word-pictures, while her family portraits – of Aunt Alexandra, Francis, Uncle Jack – are equally incisive. She is precocious, a quality partly developed by her wide reading before she goes to school. Her pictures of school are done with satirical verve but, as she comes to understand more, so they are informed with her father's compassion. For example, there is the way she handles the incident with Walter Cunningham, and her sight of the teacher with her head buried in her hands. Her reactions are a clever blend of innocence – her becoming engaged to Dill and admitting him unsexually to her bed – and experience – her visit to Calpurnia's church and her realization that Calpurnia has another life away from the Finch household. Scout can be impertinent, and she is lightly caned in school for this. She can also be aggressive – consider her fights with Jem, Cecil Jacobs and Francis, all of which suggest a quick temper which she learns to control in the light of her father's influence. Scout suffers formal education with little grace, comforted by the fact that her real education takes place at home. She learns tolerance, understanding, compassion and remorse, the latter particularly with regard to Boo Radley. She is resilient, applying the theory of relativity to her own romance with Dill, and although she wears 'britches' under her dress, the missionary tea provides her with a taste of what it is going to be like to be a lady. There is no bitterness or rancour in Scout, although she admits to feeling 'cheated' at school by living through 'twelve years of unrelieved boredom'. She learns self-discipline though and responds to Calpurnia's natural generosity of spirit. She is adventurous, taking (when she is allowed to) equality with the boys in their dares, as on the night visit to the Radley house and the incident with the tyre. Here her sensitivity is involved again, for she hears someone laughing in the house and wants to quit the game. Scout has courage. Sensing the ominous meaning of the men talking to Atticus, she reveals that she has a potential lawyer's capacity by talking Walter Cunningham's father out of continuing with their threatened action. Scout is healthy – the range of food mentioned, and Aunt Alexandra's talent as a cook show that Scout has the natural appetites of youth – and to these appetites there is added a gathering awareness of the onset of adolescence in herself and, more particularly, in Jem. She is close to him, though aware that they are growing apart and that she herself is 'getting more like a girl every day'. Her identification with Jem is shown most movingly when he goes to retrieve his pants from the Radleys in the middle of the night and she waits in fear and trepidation for his return. She does her best to adopt Atticus's maxim of climbing into another person's skin and walking around in it, and applies this principle to Jem. Scout is excitable and volatile. She screams at her first sight of snow. She is so obsessed by the Radleys that her 'stomach turned to water' when she learns that it was Boo Radley who placed the blanket around her. Scout needs warmth, sympathy, understanding, and this is supplied when she crawls into her father's lap and listens to his wisdom. She is honourable, but fallible. She won't tell tales when Francis baits her by insulting her father, but she is also an adept eavesdropper, listening in on the adult world and catching the truth and many barely understood remarks. She finds Jem's adolescent pangs difficult, but is aware of changes in herself. When Dill reaches up to kiss her, she notes 'the longing we sometimes felt each other feel' and, despite the news of Tom Robinson's death, she goes on helping at the missionary ladies' tea, knowing that she is expected to grow up to be a lady and rather relishing this initiation into the part.

The child Scout is ignorant of many things, but she loves reading and shows this when she feels like running away from school because she has been taught to read before the decreed time. She is also highly imaginative and joins the other children as they enact chapters of their story of 'One Man's Family', the Radley fantasy which evolves from their reading. The curious title of this is ironically appropriate to themselves, although they don't realize it. Scout's reading and imagination are balanced by a friendly, outgoing, sometimes courteous nature, which make her appreciate Miss Maudie, Calpurnia and little Walter Cunningham. She has a natural interest in people and events, and bears her experiences back to Atticus, who often evaluates them for her. She has spirit and independence, a boyish capacity for rough and tumble, but she is also vulnerable and 'only a girl', as we are made to realize when the chicken wire and Boo Radley save her from death. Since Scout's experiences, reactions and observations run the length of the novel, extended treatment here would be out of place. The sensitive reader will respond to and investigate the quality of her observation, her imagination, her spirit, and will try to trace the family likeness between herself, Atticus and Jem. There is, I think, an admirable consistency in their portrayal, the traits of one reflected in the traits of the others. This psychological consistency is one of the main marks of good writing in fiction.

JEM

Jem is recognizably like Scout, but also different because of the difference in age between them. Jem is nine when the retrospect opens and twelve when it ends. He is very keen to succeed at football, is imaginative and the natural leader in their games. He is so aware of masculine superiority that when Scout goes to school he patronizes her. Before, they had been far closer. Jem is surveying her reactions from the vantage point of having gone through all that Scout will experience, and having come out on the other side with a stoical acceptance that it was all necessary. His reaction to Dill is initially contemptuous, but Dill, having seen the film *Dracula*, gains instant respect in Jem's eyes and instant admission to their games as well. Jem fosters the fantasy about the Radley house, is dared into walking past it and touching it, and also undertakes the night excursion which leads to him leaving his pants on the wire. This is almost the first step in Jem's real education, for he later finds his pants neatly folded and mended, and he ponders on this just as he is forced to ponder on the presents left for the children in the tree trunk. He is always questioning Atticus about things. First he considers growing up to be a lawyer, then rejects this. He goes back to the idea and is adept at holding his own cross-examinations, almost as if he is consciously in training. He stops Scout from beating up Walter Cunningham, gets on better with Calpurnia than Scout does, but has a protective attitude towards his sister which is seen in miniature when she chews the Wrigley's Double-Mint from the tree-hole. This need to protect Scout is seen more clearly when he walks with her to and from the pageant on the night of the attack. After Scout teases him about Hot Steams, he has his revenge by awarding her first ride in the tyre to the Radley house, pushing it strongly enough to make sure that she gets there. This shows his pride, and that the 'slow fuse' Scout describes him as having (it is an apt description of his father too and demonstrates the family likeness) can be lit quite suddenly. Jem organizes the fantasies, always plays the 'born hero', and is evasive when Atticus questions him. He feels obliged to put Scout down from time to time, telling her that she's 'only a girl', and calling her 'Miss Priss'. Caught in the act of trying to torment Boo Radley, Jem, as the oldest of the three, is told off by Atticus, and, in his injured pride, undertakes the night excursion. The sudden shotgun blast causes him to lose his pants, but he has the courage to go back later that night to retrieve them. He is seriously worried when he gets them, feeling that somebody was reading his mind (ironically, Arthur Radley has made the leap, and must have been walking around inside Jem's skin, for he put the pants back knowing how worried Jem would be) but he is thrilled when he finds the pocket-watch. Later he realizes that the tree which Mr Nathan says is dying is not, and Scout finds that he is crying. Perhaps it is that he sees the whole pathos of the Radley situation, and is moved to tears by the thought of the prisoner in the house. Jem's imagination is shown again in the construction of the snowman. He protects Scout as they watch the burning of Miss Maudie's house, and then reveals how the Radley affair has eaten into him by blurting out his fears of Mr Nathan and so revealing the children's fantasies. Jem learns to admire Atticus – the one-shot Finch his son didn't know about – when he shoots Tim Johnson. Jem is afterwards in a state of 'numb confusion' and admires his father for not speaking about his talent. He decides that Atticus is a gentleman, just like Jem himself! This is a deliberate paralleling by Harper Lee of the brother–sister destiny, for Scout, despite her britches, comes to know that she is to be a lady.

Jem's positive education has been referred to in the previous section. He cuts off the tops of Mrs Dubose's camellias, reads to her as a punishment, and has a camellia bequeathed to him when she dies. He learns to realize the suffering of the old lady and, too late, the quality of her courage to which his father refers. His growing pains are reflected in his moods – he is aware that Scout *is* a girl and wants her to behave like one – his appetite and, above all, his awareness of the difficulties of the trial. Before that there is the added stress of having Aunt Alexandra look after them, and this brings out a 'maddening superiority' in Jem which leads to a fight with Scout. Jem also has his father's courage, and won't go home when his father is threatened by Mr Cunningham and his friends. He sees the court case through, though he is seriously upset by what he hears, particularly as he knows that all the evidence is on Tom Robinson's side. He begs his father to be allowed to stay in court for the verdict, discusses the law on rape with Reverend Sykes, and then weeps with anger and disbelief at the verdict. Miss Maudie cuts him a larger slice of cake than the other two get as an acknowledgement of his manhood and suffering. Jem probes Atticus in good lawyer fashion later by asking why local people weren't on juries, why women like Miss Maudie weren't either, and then learning that one member of the jury was for acquittal. But the fact that Jem is still a growing and aware boy is evident when, after all the crises, he wants Scout to examine the hairs on his chest. He goes on questioning events, coming to the conclusion that Boo Radley wants to stay inside. He is being educated in humanity, and his maturity makes him want to be responsible for Scout on the night of the pageant. In fact, Scout comes to appreciate Jem more and more, particularly as he is sympathetic rather than critical when she muffs her lines in the pageant. He protects her, stays with her, and bears the brunt of the murderous assault himself. Jem grows in reason and feeling throughout the novel, and is complementary to Scout in his own moral development.

AUNT ALEXANDRA

The other members of Atticus's family, like many of the characters in the novel, are more caricatures than real people. This is not a statement of denigration, for Harper Lee's ability to convey strongly one or two distinctive and colourful traits rather than the rounded person is apparent. Aunt Alexandra is married, but one could hardly call Uncle Jimmy a real husband, and she looks after her grandson Francis at Christmas while his parents enjoy themselves. (Francis can be quickly disposed of. He is an unpleasant tell-tale who teases Scout and baits her about her father being a nigger-lover. He then says that she called him a 'whore-lady' and assaulted him. He cries and asks his grandmother to protect him when Scout hits him in revenge for his taunt.) Alexandra has firm ideas about the status of the Finch family and about bringing Scout up as a lady. She is critical of other families because of their supposed inferiority and because they have infirmities which she defines as 'Streaks'. She delights in organizing and being bossy, trying to persuade Atticus, without success, to get rid of Calpurnia, and she is certainly a snob, delighting to promote missionary circle activities and to have tea parties for her co-religionists at the Finch house. One turns out differently from what she had expected, for when her brother comes with the news of Tom Robinson's death she is shocked and concerned – as indeed she had been throughout the trial – by the emotional and physical strain imposed on Atticus by his electing to defend a negro.

If the novel is about the education of Scout and Jem, it is also about the education of Alexandra, who blames herself for the attack on Atticus's children. In fact, she is so overcome by this that she has to leave, though not before she has indicated (her sense of propriety never in abeyance) that they might be better discussing the killing of Bob Ewell in the 'living-room'. In this crisis she is undeniably and warmly, even unobtrusively, good, unwinding the crushed wire from around Scout, and thoughtfully, kindly, sitting by Jem's bed when Scout takes Arthur Radley home. She responds to crisis, and reveals herself to be truly Atticus's sister, so that we cannot help but speculate on what frustrations lie behind her private façade.

UNCLE JACK

Uncle Jack is an essentially likeable character. He has a marvellous game of proposal–non-proposal of marriage with Miss Maudie and he is interested warmly in Scout, though he disapproves of her language and tomboyish reactions. Nonetheless he finds out the truth of her assault on Francis after Scout felt he had let her down. Uncle Jack is a doctor, and deftly removes a splinter from Scout's foot without her knowing. He admits to knowing little about children when Scout has accused him of not hearing two sides of the question, but she admires him greatly for not breaking his promise to her: he doesn't tell Atticus why it was that Scout hit Francis.

CALPURNIA

Calpurnia (another Roman connection, for the original Calpurnia was the wife of Julius Caesar) is the mother to the motherless family. At first she and Scout do not get on well. She slaps Scout for her disobedience and cheek, but watches over her charges protectively and possessively, and even establishes a code of manners of which Atticus himself would approve when she reprimands Scout for daring to be critical of Walter Cunningham's table manners. Like her son Zeebo she has acquired some education through reading Atticus's books on law, and she is obviously very fond of the children, spoiling them occasionally with cookies. Atticus depends on her and she makes no emotional demands on him. A negress in a white man's house, she seems to have successfully bridged the racial gap (this is never satisfactorily explained) though Scout notices that she talks 'nigger talk' to the negroes and speaks another language in the Finch home. Calpurnia shows presence of mind in the Tim Johnson incident, and contributes to the children's wider education by taking them to the negro church. Here she encounters some opposition from Lula to her bringing the white children, but she summarily puts her down in the best Hollywood tradition. No one must come between her and the children she regards as her special responsibility. That responsibility is shown, though rather too late, in the trial scene, when with some nerve (and, we suspect, some enjoyment of her position) she makes straight for Atticus in the courtroom in order to tell him that his children are missing. Duty is her by-word, and Atticus's dependence on her unquestioning loyalty is shown when he asks her to accompany him to Helen Robinson's house to break the news of Tom's death.

DILL

The other member of the family – I use the word deliberately – is Dill, who comes one summer and irradiates the children's lives by the quality of his imagination and participation in their games, particularly the dramas which he orchestrates, his centre-piece being the idea of making Boo Radley 'come out'. Small for his age, eccentrically dressed (later he says he wants to be a clown, but he is already one at the outset), precocious and travelled, Dill is a pathetic instance of a child whose parents do not want him. He stays with his Aunt Rachel in Maycomb. When his mother remarries, he appears to get on with his stepfather, but this is only temporary, and he runs away on one occasion and hides in Scout's room. His finest moment is when he 'hatches one', a saving lie which stops them all from getting into trouble after they had stolen off to the Radley house. Dill pretends that the reason why Jem has no pants is because he has been playing strip poker (with matchsticks) with him. Scout becomes his girl – occasionally they reach out to kiss one another – but despite all his precocity Dill is curiously innocent, relegating or ignoring sex in order to dream dreams about where babies come from. He is very sensitive, his reaction to Mr Gilmer's cross-examination makes him feel physically sick, so that he has to go outside the court where, fortunately, the Coca-Cola drinking Mr Dolphus Raymond helps to bring him round (pp. 204–5). Dill also registers, in graphic narration to Scout, the collapse of Helen Robinson as she reads the news of her husband's death in Atticus's face. Dill's reaction to the gossiping women after the trial is that he is going to be a clown, but with a difference. He will stand 'in the middle of the ring and laugh at the folks' (p. 220). Sensitive, sympathetic, bewildered by the overturning of standards in the adult 'game', Dill, like Jem, looks to Atticus with respect, and finds there the rock of comfort he needs in a bad world.

MISS MAUDIE ATKINSON

Of the other characters in *To Kill a Mockingbird* the most lovable is certainly Miss Maudie Atkinson. She and Atticus are the twin mirrors of sanity and tolerance, and they respect and love each other with uncomplicated and sure insight. On her side it is a clear recognition of his qualities; on his, a sympathetic affinity with the independent maiden lady whose voice can be acid when religious or local narrowness is on display. Maudie cares for the children, and when Scout finds herself cut out from the boys' games, she spends many pleasant hours on Miss Maudie's porch listening to her views on life, which are straight, sincere, and sympathetic. She cannot stand hypocrisy and humbug, whether it be in the narrow attitudes of the religious sects like the missionary circle, or in the celebrations which precede the trial of Tom Robinson which she calls a 'Roman carnival'. For Scout, Miss Maudie is the respected interpreter of her father's actions, explaining not only that he is 'civilized in his heart', but also that his private and public actions are the same, in other words stressing to the child the complete integrity of the man. She has a wicked sense of humour, as when she asks Miss Stephanie why she didn't invite Boo Radley into her bed, and she despises gossip or any encroachment on other people's lives. Again, she is so individualized as to be the genuine eccentric of the novel. She doesn't mind how ridiculous she appears, and always counters Jack Finch's annual public proposal of marriage by yelling back across the street at him. Another mark of her difference is her attitude to the fire at her house. She says she had always wanted a smaller house anyway. Her main concern is for her plants – and the weeds – but she has a central moral function in the novel. Although she can be effectively acid, Miss Maudie exerts a positive influence on the children by not descending to the level of prejudice, by acting as a mother figure. This is particularly so after the trial, when the children are in need of creature comforts to raise their morale. Here she reveals her sensitivity, cutting Jem a larger piece of cake than the rest in acknowledgement of his maturity, which has just been called into question by his tearful reaction to the verdict. She explains the distinction between a 'foot-washing' Baptist like old Mr Radley and her own plain religion, which is based on the kind of humanity so evident in Atticus. Her diction can be 'deadly', and she makes great play with her 'bridgework' – her clarity and directness entertain the children – but with adults she is either quietly supportive (as with Alexandra as she worries over what the trial has done to her brother) or sarcastic (as she is with Mrs Merriweather and her rooted bigotry and unchristian judgements). Miss Maudie is totally sympathetic from the reader's point of view. She may be a little larger than life, but she is of life, a voice of sanity and compassion where there are few such. She has some of the finest 'lines' in her scenes, and her 'baby-step' sounds a note of optimism for the future.

MRS DUBOSE

I have said that most of the other characters apart from the main three are caricatures, but this is not meant to detract either from their personal qualities or the impact they have on the reader. Mrs Dubose, present for one chapter, is vividly, sordidly yet sympathetically drawn. She is the mistress of invective, but it conceals the depth of her suffering. Scout's physical descriptions of her as Jem reads *Ivanhoe* to her are minute in their revolting details, yet while we feel repugnance we also feel compassion and admiration. Mrs Dubose provides direct education in feelings for the children whose father goes to law 'for niggers', and we feel that her bequest of the camellia to Jem is not an act of sadistic pleasure but rather one of deliberate and thoughtful pointing the way. Mrs Dubose has no beauty left, though her courage, beautiful in its way, irradiates her memory for Atticus and, perhaps, his children.

MISS STEPHANIE

Miss Stephanie is a pure caricature, a gossip who fosters the children's Radley fantasies by her ability to devour half-truths and expand them into lies. After the trial, and particularly after Bob Ewell spits in Atticus's face, she is frightened at the thought of possible violence and scandal. She engages Scout in conversation at the missionary circle tea, is suspicious of her irony about being a lady, but virtually takes a back seat under the immediate dominance of Mrs Merriweather.

MRS MERRIWEATHER

Mrs Merriweather is the great, organ-voiced talker about distant causes. J. Grimes Everett, having innocently supplanted her husband, whom she 'sobered up' earlier in life, is her main topic at the missionary tea. Again, she only appears in one chapter, and the pageant part of another, but her dominating devoutness reduces everybody except Miss Maudie to ignorant acquiescence. She talks of Christianity without understanding the practical application of the term to the negroes, advocates forgiveness without possessing the spirit to undertake it, mentions her own 'sulky darky', and refers to the 'good but misguided' people in Maycomb. Her pageant for the celebration of Halloween is ridiculous in the extreme. She mistranslates – for the benefit of what Scout calls the 'rustic' elements – its pompous Latin title, and her conception of each child being one of the agricultural products of Maycomb County at this time of depression is insensitive and inappropriate in the extreme. Scout's late entrance almost upstages her, and we feel that she deserves it. Mrs Merriweather is, finally, a cloying hypocrite.

ARTHUR 'BOO' RADLEY

Arthur Radley is a virtually silent presence throughout the novel. Recluse and prisoner, Arthur's main contact with the outside world is through the children he watches play and who, in imagination and fact, are trying to make him come out: come out of the house as far as they are concerned, and out of himself as far as he is concerned.

The mystery of Arthur contributes to the tension. Condemned by his past single act against the law – and this is dubious, and is obviously meant to parallel Tom Robinson's plight – Arthur is released to his family and misses the best education in the county, that of the industrial school. Rumours, largely fuelled by Miss Stephanie, circulate about him, and after the death of his father, his elder brother Nathan arrives to look after him.

Now in his thirties, Arthur leaves presents for the children, laughs at their games, mends Jem's pants and places a blanket around Scout's shoulders. All these actions anticipate his final and effective demonstration of his concern for them, when he saves Jem's life, kills Bob Ewell and helps to save Scout. At first she doesn't recognize him, but when she does she, the child, takes the big child home, though not before he has blessed Jem in a timid but moving gesture (p. 282).

His family are strict Baptists. They communicate little with their neighbours, and Mr Nathan fires his shotgun at a 'white nigger' (in reality Jem). They are responsible for Arthur's state of mind and his lopped life, and as such they contradict the main theme of the novel – humanitarian action on behalf of others – to which Arthur so movingly subscribes. The Radleys condition themselves and their own.

MAYELLA

Mayella is in part at least conditioned by economic circumstances. She is lonely and turns to a negro who has helped her and, by her standards, shown her some warmth. She has to work hard raising the motherless children, is regularly beaten and almost certainly sexually assaulted by her frequently drunken father. She has only her geraniums to live for. She breaks the Southern code, is caught in the act by her father, cannot of course face the disgrace of what she has done, and makes up her story of rape, doubtless incited to do so by the unscrupulous Bob Ewell. She covers her guilt, or tries to. She is not examined by a doctor to see if she has been raped, she tries to win Judge Taylor's and the court's sympathy by complaining that Atticus is mocking her, has an outburst which is calculated to bring every red-blooded white man to her lying side, and then refuses to answer any more of Atticus's questions. She is guilty and knows it, yet when she looks at Tom Robinson it is as if he is dirt beneath her feet. She is a pathetic and deprived person, bowed down by the circumstances of a degraded family life, with no outlet for any warmth of nature she may possess. It injures Atticus to injure her, and we share his compassion.

BOB EWELL

Nurture, or rather the lack of it, has made Mayella what she is. Nature makes her the one member of the Ewell family for whom we can feel, but our sympathy is turned back upon her by the code which insists that it is wrong to feel for a black man. We have seen that Burris Ewell's lice represent the disease inherent in the family, and this is seen in its worst form in his father. That little bantam cock Bob Ewell, aggressively pleased at being in the spotlight in court, has degraded his daughter, committed perjury, beaten his children, drunk away his relief cheques and, finally realizing that men in their hearts know that he is a liar, incestuous, and brutal almost beyond relief. He determines to exact his revenge. He follows Helen Robinson, attempts to enter Judge Taylor's house, and elsewhere we have referred to the cunning and cowardice of his attack on the children. His language offends Judge Taylor, his statements affront justice, his ignorance is despicable and 'convicts' him when he demonstrates that he is left-handed. But we must not forget that social conditions and poverty have helped to make him what he is. We hate him, but we must apply Atticus's maxim to him. Getting into Bob Ewell's skin would be unhygienic but salutary. Society owes him more than condemnation, and the humane message of the novel is that the Bob Ewells of this world must be changed by love, by humanity and by compassion.

MINOR CHARACTERS IN MAYCOMB

Miss Rachel is Dill's God-fearing aunt who takes him in every summer. Miss Tutti and Miss Frutti Barber are eccentrics (and deaf ones at that) who are subjected to a trick by the local children (Scout denies being one of them). Their furniture is stolen and hidden in their own spacious cellar. They insist on Mr Tate getting out the bloodhounds, which are brought down by him and then howl at the cellar door. In a way, this is an innocent (though unpleasant) Halloween joke which contrasts with the menacing behaviour of Bob Ewell.

Both teachers in the novel are something of caricatures. Miss Caroline Fisher is a 'peppermint drop' who has to endure Scout's ability to read before her time and before the system can change her, and Burris Ewell's cooties, as well as his aggression on his only day of attendance. Obviously her pupils are too much for her, and she ends the day with her head buried in her hands. The second teacher, Miss Gates, has a minor symbolic value underlying the main theme. She talks about Hitler persecuting the Jews but has her own intransigent views about the guilt and inferiority of the negroes. The implication is that although she is educated, she quite happily babbles about Democracy and Dictatorship without realizing her own 'persecuting' views.

There are a few characters who are influenced by Atticus and others who have moral codes of their own. Of these the least convincing is Reverend Sykes, the minister of the negro First Purchase Methodist Church. He is idealized caricature, exhorting his brethren to pray for Helen Robinson and extorting money from them for practical help. He talks sympathetically and preaches vehemently (but predictably), and is greatly concerned for Scout when she sits with him and the other negroes on the coloured balcony – he doesn't like her to hear some of the evidence. When Atticus leaves he tells her to stand, thus showing his and everyone else's respect for Atticus.

Tom Robinson, the victim of prejudice, is hardly full-blooded enough to move us greatly. He represents sympathetic, helpful, quiet, law-abiding, respectable working life (in complete contrast to Bob Ewell's), and his withered left arm is of course testimony to his innocence. He dares to feel sorry for Mayella Ewell, undoubtedly tells the simple truth of what happened, and underlines exactly what it is like to be a negro who stands no chance against a white man's testimony. He runs from the Ewell house from fear not guilt. His gentleness cannot stand the confinement and hopelessness of the Enfield Prison Farm, and he is killed while trying to escape. These two negroes – Tom and Reverend Sykes – are good, almost too good, and we are left wondering if the racial divisions in the 1930s were such that Reverend Sykes, who has spirit within his church, would not express some positive dissatisfaction with the verdict. In fact the white Mr Link Deas expresses faith in Tom, and is turned out of court for doing so. He also protects Helen Robinson from Bob Ewell, and is one of the humane influences in Maycomb. After Heck Tate's evidence we should be disinclined to place him on the side of the enlightened, yet he moves over to that side after he has weighed Atticus's words and takes much more than a 'baby-step' when he decides to cover-up the killing of Bob Ewell by Arthur Radley because he knows – though the law has demonstrated differently –

that Bob Ewell the murderer has got his just deserts. His respect for Atticus is shown when he urges him to shoot Tim Johnson, and although he warns Atticus that there may be trouble when Tom Robinson is brought to the jail, we feel that in the court he will let the trial take its course. For example, he hardly reacts when Atticus questions him about the damage to Mayella's face. Obviously he listens though, and he is not surprised when Bob Ewell attacks the children, reasoning that if he could stalk an unprotected Helen Robinson, sneak about in darkness to try to get into Judge Taylor's house, he would certainly be capable of attacking two defenceless children. His handling of the situation after the attack is admirable, and shows the man behind the sheriff's persona.

One of the finest characters in the novel is Judge Taylor, who comes brilliantly alive through Scout's descriptions of him as he chews his cigar, reprimands witnesses and rules arbitrarily and strongly. His choice of Atticus to defend Tom Robinson is evidence of his support for the movement towards enlightenment. He is aware of Bob Ewell's dangerous violence, and there is one superb moment where he has to leave the Maycomb pageant, overcome with laughter by Scout's late entry as a ham. He seems to be trying to change the establishment from within, knowing, as Atticus knows, that one day those changes will come anyway.

Mr Dolphus Raymond, himself beyond the bounds of white sympathy, shows sympathy by giving the upset Dill some settling Coca-Cola to drink. He appears for part of a chapter, yet comes vividly alive for the reader because of the pathos of his situation. He lives with a coloured woman and his children, and affects to be a drunkard because that is what the whites assume that he is. He refers to the 'simple hell' that people inflict on each other. He has found that one cannot bridge the racial gap and be thought normal.

Distinctly opposed to him on racial matters is Mr Underwood, the eccentric editor who writes his own *Maycomb Tribune*, according to legend, by himself. He is very observant, supportive of Atticus (keeping the men covered with his shotgun when they come to lynch Tom Robinson) and he is outraged by the trial verdict. Tom Robinson's judicial murder moves him to write an editorial in which he refers to the 'senseless slaughter of songbirds' and thus identifies himself positively with the humanitarian philosophy of Atticus.

In a muted way the eccentric Mr Avery is loosely identified with humanitarian impulse too. Though he is ridiculous, he does help Miss Maudie on the night of the fire. Earlier the previous day the children had made the 'morphodite' snowman at least in part like him. Two other characters worthy of note are the helpful, caring, reassuring Dr Reynolds, who sets Jem's arm and is the family doctor, and Walter Cunningham, whose table manners affront Scout but whose poverty and independence move her. Walter's father pays Atticus in goods for law advice, and although the Cunninghams have a bad reputation, they are learning the quality of tolerance. Mr Cunningham virtually calls off the lynch party after Scout has talked to him and asked to be remembered to Walter, and another Cunningham on the jury is initially for the outright acquittal of Tom Robinson. The minor characters are presented with economy, are sometimes only present for a few pages in the narrative, but their physical traits and attitudes are deftly and vividly caught.

Commentary

THEMES AND THEIR TREATMENT: NARRATIVE ART

An examination of the chapter summaries and critical evaluations which accompany them will indicate the author's main concerns in the novel: awakening humanitarian awareness, the development of ideas of equality in spirit and practice. We see the evil and immoral effects of prejudice in the small community and in the world at large. The narrative techniques are designed to present experiences as they occurred at a particular time in the childhood of Jean Louise Finch (Scout), the author's recall noting the adult reactions of the child, but adding to them the perspective of adult wisdom. The main areas covered are the domestic (the children within their home), the local (the children playing, school, neighbours, the trial and its repercussions) and the wider perspective of selected national and international events.

Fiction is not simple autobiography, however, and it would be idle speculation to identify Scout with Harper Lee. But first-person narration is a form of narrative technique which often sets up a strong and sympathetic affinity between the teller and the reader. We respond to Scout as she responds to experience, because events and people are immediate and felt. As Scout learns so we learn, and the mature narrator's evaluation enhances and extends our understanding of events.

FAMILIES

The theme of the education of the feelings and the mind is reinforced by moral, social and economic emphases. Dill is from a broken marriage and desperately needs the security of home and love. He finds it, somewhat aggressively concealed in Aunt Rachel, but positively offered by Scout, Jem and the father-figure, Atticus, to whom Dill movingly and silently registers his gratitude by carrying Atticus's chair home after the threatening incident outside the jail.

The Ewell family are conditioned morally, socially and economically by the deprivation they endure, the lice in Burris Ewell's hair symbolizing their inability to escape from its effects and perhaps too the fact that they breed moral and physical diseases, like prejudice, loneliness, aggression and murder. They live in squalor and on state assistance, so that the head of the family can beat and starve his children and sexually degrade his daughter. Behind them lies another cause for their dehumanization – the death of the mother, so that Mayella Ewell, who dares to kiss a negro, is the abused mother figure, skivvy, isolated with them all, her geraniums the pathetic symbol of escape from her present existence. Atticus too has lost a wife, but here Harper Lee works an effective contrast, for Atticus, so to speak, has gained a *real* mother for his children, and they are conditioned not only by his enlightened tolerance but by Calpurnia's domestic role and rule. Here the difference between black and white is not even considered, a sure pointer to the major themes of the novel. The provision of sympathy is the keynote. Dill has his adoptive family to turn to, Mayella has no one and, in desperation more than lust, turns to a negro and breaks the Southern code of womanhood, while Scout, from beginning to end, has Atticus's lap.

THE FUNCTION OF THE COLOURED CHARACTERS

The main themes therefore are the movements towards humanity and the rejection of prejudice, the movements – what Miss Maudie calls 'steps' – being shown in characters like Heck Tate and Mr Cunningham. One writer has described Atticus's codes as a kind of woolly liberalism, and the blacks as stereotypical descendants of those in *Uncle Tom's Cabin*, a famous, sentimental novel about slavery. There is little need to consider the first charge, which is refuted by Atticus's private and public actions in the service of others and his children. This suggests a broad tolerance but also a clear knowledge of what the future holds, a whiplash of black power in reaction to white suppression. But it must be allowed that the visit to the negro church, Calpurnia's exchange with Lula, the Reverend Sykes's coercion of his congregation into giving more money for Helen Robinson and, above all, his telling the children to stand like everybody else because their father is passing, all smack of sentimental idealism. Admittedly, these incidents support the humanitarian theme. Calpurnia tells Scout that she talks 'nigger-talk' when she is in her community, and this approximates, but in a limited way, to stepping into the shoes of others and walking around in their skins. Zeebo's 'linin'' is expressive of the pathos and deprivation of the negroes, the fact that they are not taught to read underpinning the fact that just as there is one law for black and one law for white, so there is one education for white and none for black. The description of Tom Robinson and the idiom he uses are somewhat false. He has dared to help a white woman – thus demonstrating what Aunt Alexandra would call his Humanitarian Streak – but all that the trial produces from the coloured balcony is an 'angry muffled groan' when Bob Ewell declares that he saw 'that black nigger yonder ruttin' on my Mayella!' (p. 176). The implication is important. It means that none of the negroes present would dream of using the forceful language of the white man, that none of them would lie, that none of them would offend against a code of behaviour prescribed but not observed by their white superiors. Even Calpurnia, likeable and voluble as she is, and certainly a thematic necessity, derives more from the Hollywood stereotype of the 'black-servant-with-a-heart-of-gold-who-knows-her-place'. Her visit to the court in search of her charges bears the stamp of contrivance.

THE 'MOCKINGBIRD' SYMBOL

In literature, a symbol is something used by a writer which stands for or suggests something else, and it can be associated with that something – or someone – else in an explicit or subtle way. The central symbol of Harper Lee's novel is the mockingbird of its title. At first sight the title is enigmatic, but a close look at Harper Lee's literary sophistication, her considered introduction of the mockingbird at crucial points of her narrative, shows how central that title is to the content of her novel. The first and last references to the bird indicate its importance. Miss Maudie, who represents a love of nature and a hope for human nature, tells Scout (p. 96) that it is a 'sin' to kill a mockingbird. This bird puts everything into its song and does no harm to anyone. It stands for goodness, innocence, the range of its song (which embraces that of many other birds) suggesting something more than the narrow range of man in his entrenched, small-town, racially prejudiced views. At the end of the novel Scout has learned enough about humanity from her father's standards to be able to say that it would be 'sort of like shootin' a mockingbird, wouldn't it?' to imprison Arthur Radley (p. 280). Boo, like the bird, has done no harm to anyone. The mockingbird gives its song, and Boo has given his love to 'his' children, saving their lives in the process.

The first and last symbolic references are clear, but the author's use within the rest of her novel is more subtle and ironic. We can equate Boo Radley with the mockingbird, but a much firmer equation is with Tom Robinson. He has done no harm, but is found guilty of rape though demonstrably innocent, and is judicially murdered. Mr Underwood, the newspaper proprietor, fittingly compares that killing of Tom Robinson to 'the senseless slaughter of songbirds' (p. 245), thus underlining in his outspokenness the symbolic and humane theme of the novel. One 'mockingbird' is shot, while the other, Boo Radley, has no freedom to sing. But such is the resonance of the title that it is heard in character and incident throughout. Atticus is the main mockingbird figure of the novel, for his song, a song of humanity, tolerance and compassion, embraces the unvoiced and sometimes inarticulate views of those who know the right steps to take but cannot take them until they hear Atticus's 'song'. As we have seen, Heck Tate listens, and Boo Radley is not charged with the murder of Bob Ewell. Scout herself will be a 'mockingbird', listening to her father and imitating his humanity. She notes that the birds are strangely silent when Atticus shoots the mad dog, ironically in front of the house where Boo Radley lives. The birds are silent again in Scout's mind at the end of the trial scenes, almost as if she recognizes that Tom Robinson's innocence is a pathetic equivalent to that of the birds'.

The ironic use of 'mocking' which recalls the title of the novel can be further explored. On the night when the children are attacked returning from the Maycomb pageant they again hear 'a solitary mocker'. They are also pursued by one, the drunken Bob Ewell 'mocking' all standards of decency by trying to kill Atticus's children in revenge for Atticus's exposure of his (Ewell's) own degraded practices. As we have seen, the children are saved by another 'solitary mocker' in the form of Boo Radley. We remember too that in court Mayella Ewell had accused Atticus of 'mockin'' her, though, by calling her 'Miss Mayella', he is politely mocking the Southern mode of address and exposing the 'polite fiction of Southern womanhood', even if it hurts him to do so.

The trial itself is a form of mockery, the jurors 'mocking' justice by condemning an innocent man. The ladies' missionary tea is a mockery of true Christianity, and Zeebo's 'linin'' of the hymns a plaintive (and innocent) mockery of the negroes' lack of education, for each member of the congregation is in effect a bird 'mocking' by imitation the leader Zeebo. The interested reader will find other instances where, without straining, the mockingbird symbol may be ironically applied, even down to the children 'mocking' the few books they have stored in their minds by making fantasies from them and, of course, their 'mocking' of Boo Radley which they regret so much later.

THE STYLE OF THE NOVEL

The style of *To Kill a Mockingbird* is finely evocative of the period. The current slang of the children, the Southern intonations of Miss Stephanie, the other ladies at the missionary tea, and the distinctive speech of the negroes like Tom Robinson and Calpurnia all contribute to give the book a colloquial appeal. For the most part it is natural, often dramatic, sometimes humorous, as when Miss Maudie tells Miss Stephanie, who has woken in the middle of the night to find Boo Radley staring at her, 'what did you do, Stephanie, move over in the bed and make room for him?' (p. 51). Maycomb may be a 'tired old town', but the reader gets the feeling of *life*, with the children observing Mr Avery urinating, making a 'morphodite' of snow, watching Miss Maudie's house burn down, sitting tensely at the trial, finding Dill concealed in their bedroom, being falsely scared by Cecil Jacobs and nearly killed by Bob Ewell. These are incidents selected from a number which show the graphic immediacy of Harper Lee's style. Its unforced naturalness makes the novel eminently readable, exciting and stimulating. The use of dialogue is particularly effective, and there is little doubt that its high standard contributed to the quality of the film which was based on the book.

Another attractive aspect of the style is the author's superb sense of narrative climax, either at the end of a chapter or at a significant point within it. An example of the first would be when Scout, at the end of Chapter Nine, overhears Atticus telling Uncle Jack about the ordeal which lies before the children in the forthcoming trial of Tom Robinson, Scout realizing many years later that he had intended her to hear every word. This kind of climax is muted in a sense, but effective because it *prepares* Scout for trouble without her fully understanding why, and the fact that she doesn't understand until later means that the tension inherent in her experiences is not diminished. The climax within the chapter is shown when it is revealed that Tom Robinson's left arm is twelve inches shorter than his right (p. 189). Most people in court know this and his innocence is thus demonstrated visually. It is a wonderfully dramatic moment, and it makes the verdict a mockery (the appropriate word), with its blatant rejection of what the eye sees and what the mind knows. One or two voices have been raised against Harper Lee's tendency to make 'our heroine' feature so much in the novel in terms of dramatic incident – as when Scout talking to Mr Cunningham averts an attack on Atticus and Tom Robinson – but the level of her writing never sinks into the schoolgirl adventure category. She tells a good story – here a series of good stories – but the literary control and the structural organization of her novel join the strands of the story, so that there are no loose ends.

There is at times a literary self-consciousness, the influence of the adult behind the child, with references to Mr Jingle, Hodge, or broader historical references which embrace Confederate generals in the Civil War and Lord Melbourne, Prime Minister of England when Queen Victoria came to the throne. In fact, the range of reference and general learning contribute to the authenticity of the novel and the references in no way impede its narrative flow, nor are they produced ostentatiously for our edification. Rather, they enhance our appreciation since they come from the child, Scout, and are often not fully grasped or understood. But there is one area of literary experience which is very skilfully used by the author, and this concerns the books read by the children and dramatized by them into Radley fantasies. Their authors – with names like Oliver Optic, Victor Appleton and Edgar Rice Burroughs (best known for the Tarzan books) – provide the inspiration for the children's plays. Ironically, they are all boys' writers, and they play some part in conditioning Scout into being a tomboy, though she often gets the worst parts. There is further irony in this reading, for the dramas they enact are seen in relation to the real drama going on around them and in which they become involved. But even at the end of the novel, when she has been almost killed, Scout reverts to *The Grey Ghost*, by Seckatary Hawkins, as if life hadn't anything more exciting to offer. Perhaps this reaction is natural, since Scout is only a child and is reverting to the security of the stories she knows, a refuge – like Atticus's lap – from the real life experiences which, for much of the time, she only half understands. But Scout is educated through life, and her progression is given a full psychological consistency throughout the novel.

RELIGION AND EDUCATION

To Kill a Mockingbird offers a close and somewhat satirical look at man's misguidedness not just in matters of colour prejudice but in the areas of education and religion.

The treatment of education is overtly satirical, for the kind of education the children receive has little relation to their everyday lives. The major theme of the novel is the education of the feelings in humanitarian awareness, and the failure of the state school system to provide any positive direction here is given a considered treatment in Chapter Twenty-Six, where Miss Gates sings the praises of democracy as against the dictatorship of Hitler, asserting that 'we don't believe in persecuting anybody' (p. 249). This is manifestly hypocritical in view of her attitude towards the negroes. The ritual utterance of words like 'democracy' and 'prejudice' shows the author indicating the complete unawareness of those who believe they live in an enlightened way, when, on their doorstep, they are denying democracy and displaying prejudice.

The attack on religious hypocrisy is sustained throughout and obviously supports the humanitarian theme of the novel. The Radleys have imprisoned Boo for a youthful misdemeanour rather than let him acquire an education and be further tempted in the outside world. The 'foot-washing' Baptists are epitomized by this determined repression: their saving Boo from sin by committing the unforgivable sin of denying him life. The Radleys' co-religionists drive into Maycomb in a wagon for the trial – obviously displaying Christian concern that justice should be done – but run into a verbal retort from Miss Maudie which causes them to speed on.

But Harper Lee's main satire of religious people is saved for the ladies' missionary circle. First, they spend much time talking of food, discussing the delicacies prepared by what Mrs Merriweather would call 'the darky in the kitchen', and this is grossly unchristian when we recall the times of economic depression in which they are living. Secondly, they gossip interminably and uncharitably, so that the occasion cannot be dignified by any spiritual concern. That concern is expressed through Mrs Merriweather's loquacious and gushing account of the missionary activity of J. Grimes Everett in a distant jungle, her identification with the far-away rather than the immediate problems under her nose. Those under the noses of the missionary ladies are swept aside with scant attention to Christian principles, Mrs Merriweather saying that Scout is lucky to be living in a Christian town with Christian people, that the preacher ought to ensure that Helen Robinson leads a Christian life, and that if they let the negroes know that they 'forgive 'em' (presumably for daring to criticize a flagrantly dishonest verdict against Tom Robinson) everything will blow over. The satire is enhanced by Scout's account of the similarity of their clothes and cosmetics, for this essentially comfortable conformity has its own distinctive badge of respectability, so that Miss Maudie, invited because she is a neighbour, is able to break the circle temporarily by an icy comment, but of course it will not hinder the flow of prejudice.

Another effective device is to have reality thrust itself into the narrative, for Atticus comes to tell Miss Maudie, Alexandra and Scout that Tom Robinson has been shot. This dramatic news contrasts with what is merely talk in the dining-room. Thus those who should be practising immediate and practical Christianity where it is most needed, because of inherited and conditioned prejudice, have degraded both themselves and their religion.

FIGURATIVE LANGUAGE

Figurative language, often with symbolic overtones, is used throughout *To Kill a Mockingbird*. Sometimes it contributes to the sense of pattern and order of the novel, as when Scout waits for Atticus to shoot Tim Johnson and thinks that he is moving like an underwater swimmer (p. 102). This image recurs to her when she is watching the jury return to give their verdict in the trial, and she associates them immediately with Atticus and the shooting. This not only gives Scout's inner thoughts a degree of consistency, it also establishes a sub-conscious connection between one killing – necessary – and another which is about to be set in motion: the judicial killing of Tom Robinson. There is also much vivid and figurative description. Mrs Dubose's mouth, which seems to work independently of the rest of her, is 'like a clam hole at low tide' (p. 113), while the wet 'inched like a glacier' down her face (p. 112). Aunt Alexandra is compared to Mount Everest, Miss Maudie is a 'chameleon lady', and the shadow of Nathan Radley on the porch is described as 'crisp as toast'. These images, which are never inappropriate or contrived, make the novel a deft and economical one. Added to these imaginative comparisons are some delightfully ironic touches from the mature writer behind the child: Miss Caroline Fisher's teaching of the Dewey Decimal System is referred to as 'impressionistic revelations' (p. 24), Scout refers to her 'noontime fall from grace' (p. 34) and also says that she was 'weary from the day's crimes' (p. 35), a kind of wry hyperbole (or exaggeration) which indicates that not much has in fact happened. When Miss Maudie finds nut-grass she clears it with a poisonous substance and Scout compares its effect to the 'Second Battle of the Marne'.

Clichés in *To Kill a Mockingbird* are rare (except for the clichés of ordinary, everyday speech, which are a form of realism), but occasionally the imagery is rather cloying and commonplace, as when Maycomb is compared to 'an island in a patchwork sea of cotton fields and timber land' (p. 134).

MYSTERY, THRILLERS AND SUSPENSE

There are elements of the novel which bear direct comparison with the thriller or mystery-type narrative. Harper Lee is mistress of various types of atmosphere: the atmosphere of mystery or fear, of tension and drama, of pathos and sadness, of loneliness and sordidness. As always the child's perspective is maintained. Thus, when Scout rolls in the tyre to the Radley house, she reveals at the end of the chapter that she had heard someone laughing within. The effect is to create suspense – is there something very wrong within the Radley house? Are the children's fantasies somewhere near the truth? The reader is left in anticipation that something dramatic will happen. It does, but in a muted way, for the author is adept at placing clues at significant points in the narrative, as when the children find the effigies of themselves, or when Scout finds the blanket around her shoulders, or when she feels someone pull her attacker away from her.

The courtroom scene is redolent of tension and drama, with the cross-examination of Atticus the pivot, particularly as he leads Bob Ewell into the prepared trap by getting him to write his name, thus showing that he is left-handed, and by producing Tom Robinson at a critical juncture to display his withered left arm. Here we are aware of each character in the drama: Ewell, Atticus, Mayella, the sporadic authority of Judge Taylor and of the twelve good men who are to be untrue. Further we are aware of the silent negro watchers from their selected and separated coloured balcony, and of the children registering every moment of the biggest drama in their lives.

Once that tension is over it is succeeded by another: that of the threats of Bob Ewell, with the ominous intrusion of Judge Taylor's house, the stalking of Helen Robinson, the spitting at Atticus. All these are the prelude to the vicious attack on Scout and Jem. The high point of tension in the novel is, of course, the attack itself, which is brilliantly and ironically contrived. Here we have the darkness of the night, the boy escorting the girl because the adults do not really want to see the performance, the mock-scare (note the word) of Cecil

Jacobs, the illusory and fake scares on which they spend their nickels (the House of Horrors), Scout actually sleeping when she should have been ready to perform. There is a deft touch when the children are offered a lift home and reject it, and this is followed by another illusory experience – the fact that they think the silent follower is Cecil Jacobs. And even after the attack the tension, the pitch at which Harper Lee keeps her narrative is not allowed to die down. There is the mystery of the rescuer to be solved, the concern about Jem, the killing of Ewell and the cover-up which Atticus thinks is a cover-up for Jem, but which in reality turns out to be a cover-up for the man Atticus has always protected – Arthur Radley.

SADNESS IN THE NOVEL

Pathos and sadness, despite the generally light touch of the author, are present in particular scenes and in the mostly unseen but ever-present background figure of Arthur Radley. Again we must refer also to Mrs Dubose, and particularly to Chapter Eleven, which deals with Jem's cutting off the heads of the camellias, agreeing to read *Ivanhoe* to her as a punishment and repentance. Allied to this are Scout's observation in physical close-up of the dying Mrs Dubose, and Atticus's account of her bravery until she died, followed by Jem's almost hysterical reaction to the perfect camellia she has bequeathed to him. Here we have the last phase in the children's education before the onset of the trial, and typically Atticus discounts Jem's fear of the darkness and creepiness of the house. The children's fantasies about such things are about to be displaced by the reality of suffering and loneliness.

Loneliness and isolation, certainly present in Mrs Dubose, are exemplified in Mayella Ewell, but more terribly and pessimistically. It is impossible for Mayella Ewell's feelings to be educated. Living on the poverty line where shoes are made out of tyre strips, where her father drinks and beats the rest of the children and abuses her, where whites give her what Scout calls the back of their hand, and where negroes won't mix with her because she is white, she has no future in the kind of society depicted by Harper Lee in Maycomb. Her attempts to keep clean, her treasuring of the geraniums, the responsibility for children with perpetual colds and ground-itch, the pathetic reaching out towards Tom Robinson, all these ironically underline the main theme of the novel – the education of the feelings towards humanity. They reveal them in a negative and hopeless way. For Scout, Jem, Dill, there is a positive future. Their economic and moral circumstances ensure hope. For Mayella there is no future beyond the present, and the present will not change. Tom Robinson's reflex of kindness towards Mayella ironically leads to his own tragedy.

Glossary

Ad Astra per Aspera: 'to the stars through harshness' (motto of Kansas State in 1861)

Alabama, Code of: a summary of the laws of the state

Appleton, Victor: author of boys' stories

Appomattox: the village in Virginia where General Grant (of the North) received the surrender of General Lee (of the South) in 1865, at the end of the American Civil War

Arlington: the National Cemetery, Washington, D.C.

Atticus: Titus Pomponius (109–32 B.C.), friend and correspondent of Cicero

Auburn: a town about 125 miles north-east of Monroeville

Aylmer, Rose: the girl in a love-poem by Walter Savage Landor (1775–1864)

Baldwin County: situated between Mobile Bay and the boundary line with Florida

Bellingraths: beautiful gardens in Theodore, near Mobile

Birmingham: important industrial town about 140 miles north of Monroeville

Blackstone's Commentaries: by Sir William Blackstone (1723–80), these contained a body of information on law and were standard reading for many years

Bragg, Braxton: confederate general (1817–76)

bread lines: queues of poor people lining up for free food

Bryan, William Jennings: American politician (1860–1925)

Burroughs, Edgar Rice: author of the Tarzan books (1875–1950)

CSA: Confederate states of America

Cajuns: people of mixed Indian, Negro and white blood

Champertous Contrivance: in law, a claimant who assists another and is given a share of the gains as a result

Clanton: town about 90 miles north of Monroeville

cootie: head louse

Creek Nation: confederacy of Indian tribes in Georgia and Alabama before the latter became a state in 1819

Davis, Elmer: American radio broadcaster (1889–1945) and evaluator of news items

Dewey Decimal System: a way of classifying books in libraries

Dracula: film based on Bram Stoker's novel (1897)

Einstein, Albert: the celebrated physicist (1879–1955) who evolved the Theory of Relativity

ex cathedra: spoken authoritatively

flivver: a cheap car

Gothic: (a) applied to the novels of 'horror' written in the late eighteenth century, (b) style of architecture

Grady, Henry W.: journalist and speaker who advocated peace and reconciliation after the American Civil War

Grey Ghost, The: children's book by 'Seckatary Hawkins'

haint: ghost

Hodge: Samuel Johnson's cat

Holmes, Sherlock: the celebrated private detective created by Sir Arthur Conan Doyle (1859–1930)

holy-roller: person exhibiting religious frenzy

Hood: Confederate general (1831–79)

Howell, Dixie: football player for the University of Alabama

Hunt, William Holman: Pre-Raphaelite painter (1827–1910)

Indian-heads: old American one cent coins

Ivanhoe: one of the Waverley novels by Sir Walter Scott (1771–1832), written in 1819

Jackson, Andrew: seventh President of the United States (1767–1845)

Jackson, Stonewall (*Ol' Blue Light*): Confederate general (1824–63)

Jefferson, Thomas: third President of the United States (1743–1826)

Jingle: an eccentric, humorous character in Charles Dickens's *Pickwick Papers*

Jitney Jungle: amusement arcade, cheap entertainment

Ku Klux Klan: secret society opposed to the abolition of slavery

Kudzu: Chinese/Japanese plant with butterfly-shaped flowers

L & N: Louisville and Nashville

Lamb, Charles: writer and critic who wrote under the name of 'Elia' (1775–1834)

Mardi Gras: carnival held on the last day before Lent

Marne: First World War battle, northern France, 1918

Melbourne, Lord: Prime Minister of England (1778–1848)

Mennonites: Protestant sect named after their founder, Menno Simmons

Merlin: the magician of Arthurian legend

Missouri Compromise: legal bills which had to go through Congress before Missouri could become the twenty-fourth state in 1820

Mobile: chief port of Alabama, on the Gulf of Mexico

Mockingbird (*mocker*): American bird of the thrush family that mimics other birds' songs

Montgomery: state capital of Alabama

'*Morphodite*': hermaphrodite, having both male and female characteristics

Nashville: the capital of Tennessee

Optic, Oliver: pen-name of a writer of boys' stories

Pensacola: city and port of Florida on the Gulf of Mexico

philippic: speech abusive in tone

Pulitzer Prize: U.S. literary award

Rice Christians: converts to Christianity who are rewarded with goods

Rockefeller, John D.: American millionaire philanthropist (1839–1937)

roly-poly: millipede

Roosevelt, Mrs Eleanor: wife of Franklin D. Roosevelt, who was President of the United States from 1933 to 1945

Rose Bowl: the stadium which houses the final of the American football championship

Rosetta Stone: the engraved stone which helped to decipher hieroglyphics, discovered near Rosetta in the Nile delta in 1799

'*Rover Boys, The*': heroes of boys' books about school

scrip stamps: tokens issued to the poor to be exchanged for goods

Shadrach: with Meshach and Abednego, cast into the fiery furnace by Nebuchadnezzar (Daniel III: 21–3)

Swift, Tom: hero of a number of boys' books

Tuscaloosa: former state capital of Alabama

Victrola: trade name for an early gramophone

Washington: the capital of the United States

Wesley, John: founder of Methodism (1703–91)

Wheeler, Brigadier General Joe: American officer and politician (1836–1906)

Examination Questions

1. Read the following passage, and answer all the questions printed beneath it:

Calpurnia rinsed her hands and followed Jem into the yard. 'I don't see any dog,' she said.

She followed us beyond the Radley Place and looked where Jem pointed. Tim Johnson was not much more than a speck in the distance, but he was closer to us. He walked erratically, as if his right legs were shorter than his left legs. He reminded me of a car stuck in a sand-bed.

'He's gone lopsided,' said Jem.

Calpurnia stared, then grabbed us by the shoulders and ran us home. She shut the wood door behind us, went to the telephone and shouted, 'Gimme Mr Finch's office!'

'Mr Finch!' she shouted. 'This is Cal. I swear to God there's a mad dog down the street a piece – he's comin' this way, yes sir, he's – Mr Finch, I declare he is – old Tim Johnson, yes sir ... yessir ... yes –'

She hung up and shook her head when we tried to ask her what Atticus had said. She rattled the telephone hook and said, 'Miss Eula May – now ma'am, I'm through talkin' to Mr Finch, please don't connect me no more – listen, Miss Eula May, can you call Miss Rachel and Miss Stephanie Crawford and whoever's got a phone on this street and tell 'em a mad dog's comin'? Please ma'am!'

Calpurnia listened. 'I know it's February, Miss Eula May, but I know a mad dog when I see one. Please ma'am hurry!'

Calpurnia asked Jem, 'Radleys got a phone?'

Jem looked in the book and said no. 'They won't come out anyway, Cal.'

'I don't care, I'm gonna tell 'em.'

She ran to the front porch, Jem and I at her heels. 'You stay in that house!' she yelled.

Calpurnia's message had been received by the neighbourhood. Every wood door within our range of vision was closed tight. We saw no trace of Tim Johnson. We watched Calpurnia running towards the Radley Place, holding her skirt and apron above her knees. She went up to the front steps and banged on the door. She got no answer, and she shouted, 'Mr Nathan, Mr Arthur, mad dog's comin'! Mad dog's comin'!'

(i) Show how this passage brings out Calpurnia's ability to deal with an emergency.

(ii) Give one other example to show how thoroughly Calpurnia justified Atticus's confidence in her as a substitute for the children's dead mother.

(iii) Give an account of the way the problem of the mad dog was dealt with, and explain how Jem's opinion of his father was changed as a result.

(*Oxford Local Examination Board, 1981*)

2. Either (*a*) Give an account of Scout's misfortunes on her first day at school, and explain why that day must have been an ordeal for Miss Caroline, too.

Or (*b*) '. . . the court appointed him to defend this nigger.'

'Yeah, but Atticus aims to *defend* him!'

Show how skilfully Atticus builds up his defence of Tom Robinson. What prevents the jury from declaring him innocent?

(*Oxford Local Examination Board, 1981*)

3. Read the following passage, and answer all the questions printed beneath it:

Dill tried to pull himself together as we ran down the south steps. Mr Link Deas was a lonely figure on the top step. 'Anything happenin', Scout?' he asked as we went by. 'No sir,' I answered over my shoulder. 'Dill here, he's sick.'

'Come on out under the trees,' I said. 'Heat got you, I expect.' We chose the fattest live oak and we sat under it.

'It was just him I couldn't stand,' Dill said.

'Who, Tom?'

'That old Mr Gilmer doin' him thataway, talking so hateful to him –'

'Dill, that's his job. Why, if we didn't have prosecutors – well, we couldn't have defence attorneys, I reckon.'

Dill exhaled patiently. 'I know all that, Scout. It was the way he said it made me sick, plain sick.'

'He's supposed to act that way, Dill, he was cross –'

'He didn't act that way when –'

'Dill, those were his own witnesses.'

'Well, Mr Finch didn't act that way to Mayella and old man Ewell when he cross-examined them. The way that man called him "boy" all the time and sneered at him, an' looked around at the jury every time he answered –'

'Well, Dill, after all he's just a Negro.'

'I don't care one speck. It ain't right, somehow it ain't right to do 'em that way. Hasn't anybody got any business talkin' like that – it just makes me sick.'

'That's just Mr Gilmer's way, Dill, he does 'em all that way. You've never seen him get good'n down on one yet. Why, when – well, today Mr Gilmer seemed to me like he wasn't half trying. They do 'em all that way, most lawyers, I mean.'

'Mr Finch doesn't.'

'He's not an example, Dill, he's –' I was trying to grope in my memory for a sharp phrase of Miss Maudie Atkinson's. I had it: 'He's the same in the court-room as he is on the public streets.'

'That's not what I mean,' said Dill.

'I know what you mean, boy,' said a voice behind us. We thought it came from the tree-trunk, but it belonged to Mr Dolphus Raymond.

He peered around the trunk at us. 'You aren't thin-hided, it just makes you sick, doesn't it?'

(i) How did Mr Link Deas's sympathy for Tom Robinson account for his being outside the courtroom? How did he later continue to show his sympathy for the Robinson family?

(ii) What was the popular belief about Dolphus Raymond (line 36)? How did Dill discover the truth?

(iii) In what way did Atticus's treatment of Mayella (line 18) differ from Mr Gilmer's treatment of Tom? How did Mayella respond to Atticus's treatment?

(iv) What contrasts between Scout and Dill does Harper Lee bring out in this extract?

(*Oxford Local Examination Board, 1981*)

4. Either (*a*) Give an account of the day snow fell in Maycomb, and of the events of the night which followed.

Or (*b*) 'Boo was our neighbour. He gave us two soap dolls, a broken watch and chain, a pair of good luck pennies and our lives ... We had given him nothing.'

How, in the course of the novel, did Arthur Radley help the children? What did they, though unaware of it, give him in return?

(*Oxford Local Examination Board, 1981*)

5. Read the following passage, and answer all the questions printed beneath it:

They said later that Mrs Merriweather was putting her all into the grand finale, that she had crooned, 'Po-ork', with a confidence born of pine-trees and butter-beans entering on cue. She waited a few seconds, then called, 'Po-ork?' When nothing materialized, she yelled, 'Pork!'

I must have heard her in my sleep, or the band playing *Dixie* woke me, but it was when Mrs Merriweather triumphantly mounted the stage with the state flag that I chose to make my entrance. Chose is incorrect: I thought I'd better catch up with the rest of them.

They told me later that Judge Taylor went out behind the auditorium and stood there slapping his knees so hard Mrs Taylor brought him a glass of water and one of his pills.

Mrs Merriweather seemed to have a hit, everybody was cheering so, but she caught me back-stage and told me I had ruined her pageant. She made me feel awful, but when Jem came to fetch me he was sympathetic. He said he couldn't see my costume much from where he was sitting. How he could tell I was feeling bad under my costume I don't know, but he said I did all right, I just came in a little late, that was all. Jem was becoming almost as good as Atticus at making you feel right when things went wrong. Almost – not even Jem could make me go through that crowd, and he consented to wait backstage with me until the audience left.

(i) Explain as clearly as you can why Judge Taylor needed *water and one of his pills* (line 12), and why Mrs Merriweather told Scout she had *ruined her pageant* (line 14).

(ii) What, in this passage, shows that Jem is growing up?

(iii) Give a clear account of what happens to Jem and Scout from the time they leave the school until Jem is carried into the house.

6. Either (*a*) Give an account of the ways in which the children tried to make contact with Boo (Arthur Radley). How did Scout finally meet him?

Or (*b*) 'I destroyed his (Ewell's) last shred of credibility at that trial.' Show in detail how Atticus did this. Why, then, was Tom Robinson found guilty?

(*Oxford Local Examination Board, 1982*)

7. Read the following passage, and answer all the questions printed beneath it:

'. . . Robert E. Lee Ewell!'

In answer to the clerk's booming voice, a little bantam cock of a man rose and strutted to the stand, the back of his neck reddening at the sound of his name. When he turned around to take the oath, we saw that his face was red as his neck. We also saw no resemblance to his namesake. A shock of wispy new-washed hair stood up from his forehead; his nose was thin, pointed, and shiny; he had no chin to speak of – it seemed to be a part of his crepey neck.

'– so help me God,' he crowed.

Every town the size of Maycomb had families like the Ewells. No economic fluctuations changed their status – people like the Ewells lived as guests of the county in prosperity as well as in the depths of a depression. No truant officers could keep their numerous offspring in school; no public health officer could free them from congenital defects, various worms, and the diseases indigenous to filthy surroundings.

Maycomb's Ewells lived behind the town garbage dump in what was once a Negro cabin.

(i) Show in detail how the unpleasantness of Ewell is emphasized in lines 1–8 (*In answer . . . he crowed*).

(ii) Explain and bring out the humour of *the Ewells lived as guests of the county* (lines 11–12).

(iii) Contrast the impressions made by Tom Robinson and Ewell in the court.

(*Oxford Local Examination Board, 1982*)

8. Either (*a*) Give an account of the children's visit to the First Purchase African Church with Calpurnia. What new things did Scout learn on that occasion?

Or (*b*) 'Atticus is a gentleman', Jem asserted. By referring to Atticus's behaviour on a number of occasions, show how the novel supports Jem's opinion of his father.

(*Oxford Local Examination Board, 1982*)

MORE ABOUT PENGUINS, PELICANS AND PUFFINS

For further information about books available from Penguins please write to Dept EP, Penguin Books Ltd, Harmondsworth, Middlesex UB7 0DA.

In the U.S.A.: For a complete list of books available from Penguins in the United States write to Dept DG, Penguin Books, 299 Murray Hill Parkway, East Rutherford, New Jersey 07073.

In Canada: For a complete list of books available from Penguins in Canada write to Penguin Books Canada Ltd, 2801 John Street, Markham, Ontario L3R 1B4.

In Australia: For a complete list of books available from Penguins in Australia write to the Marketing Department, Penguin Books Australia Ltd, P.O. Box 257, Ringwood, Victoria 3134.

In New Zealand: For a complete list of books available from Penguins in New Zealand write to the Marketing Department, Penguin Books (N.Z.) Ltd, Private Bag, Takapuna, Auckland 9.

In India: For a complete list of books available from Penguins in India write to Penguin Overseas Ltd, 706 Eros Apartments, 56 Nehru Place, New Delhi 110019.

ENGLISH AND
AMERICAN LITERATURE

☐ *Helbeck of Bannisdale* **Mrs Humphrey Ward**   £3.50

Edited by Brian Worthington. Written in 1898, a classic to rate with the novels of George Eliot and Charlotte Brontë, this is a subtle and impressive treatment of 'the love between man and woman'.

☐ *The Red Badge of Courage* **Stephen Crane**   £1.50

Introduced by Pascal Covici, Jr. 'A psychological portrayal of fear', and one of the greatest novels ever written about war: the story of a raw Union recruit during the American Civil War.

☐ *Heart of Darkness* **Joseph Conrad**   £0.95

Conrad's most profound exploration of human savagery and despair is contained in this story of Marlowe's search for Mister Kurtz in the jungle of the Belgian Congo: a vision that has haunted readers, novelists and poets throughout the century.

☐ *Selected Writings* **Samuel Johnson**   £3.95

Edited by Patrick Cruttwell. Including generous selections from his Dictionary, his edition of Shakespeare, and his *Lives of the Poets*, plus excerpts from his journalism, letters and private prayers.

☐ *Call It Sleep* **Henry Roth**   £3.50

Published in 1934, this extraordinary novel reveals, through the eyes of David Schearl (the son of immigrant Jews), a profusion of life and family relationships in the teeming jungle of a New York City slum.

☐ *A Journey to the Western Islands of Scotland*
Johnson
The Journal of a Tour to the Hebrides **Boswell**   £3.50

Edited by Peter Levi. These two journals of their joint tour of Scotland in 1773 are masterpieces of travel-writing, human observation and glorious, sardonic wit.

PENGUIN OMNIBUSES

☐ *The Penguin Complete Sherlock Holmes*
   Sir Arthur Conan Doyle   £5.95

With all fifty-six classic short stories, plus *A Study in Scarlet*, *The Sign of Four*, *The Hound of the Baskervilles* and *The Valley of Fear*, this volume contains the remarkable career of Baker Street's most famous resident.

☐ *The Alexander Trilogy* **Mary Renault**   £4.95

Containing *Fire from Heaven*, *The Persian Boy* and *Funeral Games* – her re-creation of Ancient Greece acclaimed by Gore Vidal as 'one of this century's most unexpectedly original works of art'.

☐ *The Penguin Complete Novels of George Orwell*   £5.50

Containing the six novels: *Animal Farm*, *Burmese Days*, *A Clergyman's Daughter*, *Coming Up For Air*, *Keep the Aspidistra Flying* and *Nineteen Eighty-Four*.

☐ *The Penguin Essays of George Orwell*   £4.95

Famous pieces on 'The Decline of the English Murder', 'Shooting an Elephant', political issues and P. G. Wodehouse feature in this edition of forty-one essays, criticism and sketches – all classics of English prose.

☐ *The Penguin Collected Stories of*
   Isaac Bashevis Singer   £4.95

Forty-seven marvellous tales of Jewish magic, faith and exile. 'Never was the Nobel Prize more deserved . . . He belongs with the giants' – *Sunday Times*

☐ *Famous Trials* **Harry Hodge and James H. Hodge**   £3.50

From Madeleine Smith to Dr Crippen and Lord Haw-Haw, this volume contains the most sensational murder and treason trials, selected by John Mortimer from the classic Penguin Famous Trials series.

PENGUIN OMNIBUSES

☐ *The Penguin Complete Novels of Jane Austen* £5.95

Containing the seven great novels: *Sense and Sensibility*, *Pride and Prejudice*, *Mansfield Park*, *Emma*, *Northanger Abbey*, *Persuasion* and *Lady Susan*.

☐ *The Penguin Kenneth Grahame* £3.95

Containing his wonderful evocations of childhood – *The Golden Age* and *Dream Days* – plus his masterpiece, *The Wind in the Willows*, originally written for his son and since then loved by readers of all ages.

☐ *The Titus Books* Mervyn Peake £5.95

Titus Groan, *Gormenghast* and *Titus Alone* form this century's masterpiece of Gothic fantasy. 'It is uniquely brilliant . . . a rich wine of fancy' – Anthony Burgess

☐ *Life at Thrush Green* 'Miss Read' £3.50

Full of gossip, humour and charm, these three novels – *Thrush Green*, *Winter in Thrush Green* and *News from Thrush Green* – make up a delightful picture of life in a country village.

☐ *The Penguin Classic Crime Omnibus* £4.95

Julian Symons's original anthology includes all the masters – Doyle, Poe, Highsmith, Graham Greene and P. D. James – represented by some of their less familiar but most surprising and ingenious crime stories.

☐ *The Penguin Great Novels of D. H. Lawrence* £4.95

Containing *Sons and Lovers*, *The Rainbow* and *Women in Love*: the three famous novels in which Lawrence brought his story of human nature, love and sexuality to its fullest flowering.

PENGUIN OMNIBUSES

☐ *The Penguin Brontë Sisters*　　　　　　　　　　　£4.95

Containing Anne Brontë's *The Tenant of Wildfell Hall*, Charlotte Brontë's *Jane Eyre* and Emily Brontë's *Wuthering Heights*.

☐ *The Penguin Thomas Hardy 1*　　　　　　　　　　£4.95

His four early Wessex novels: *Under the Greenwood Tree, Far From the Madding Crowd, The Return of the Native* and *The Mayor of Casterbridge*.

☐ *The Penguin Thomas Hardy 2*　　　　　　　　　　£5.50

Containing the four later masterpieces: *The Trumpet-Major, The Woodlanders, Tess of the D'Urbervilles* and *Jude the Obscure*.

These books should be available at all good bookshops or news-agents, but if you live in the UK or the Republic of Ireland and have difficulty in getting to a bookshop, they can be ordered by post. Please indicate the titles required and fill in the form below.

NAME _____ BLOCK CAPITALS

ADDRESS _____

_____

_____

Enclose a cheque or postal order payable to The Penguin Bookshop to cover the total price of books ordered, plus 50p for postage. Readers in the Republic of Ireland should send £IR equivalent to the sterling prices, plus 67p for postage. Send to: The Penguin Bookshop, 54/56 Bridlesmith Gate, Nottingham, NG1 2GP.

You can also order by phoning (0602) 599295, and quoting your Barclaycard or Access number.

Every effort is made to ensure the accuracy of the price and availability of books at the time of going to press, but it is sometimes necessary to increase prices and in these circumstances retail prices may be shown on the covers of books which may differ from the prices shown in this list or elsewhere. This list is not an offer to supply any book.

This order service is only available to residents in the UK and the Republic of Ireland.